Dream

DESSERTS

Dream DESSERTS

60 Over-the-Top Recipes *for* Truly Fabulous Flavor

AMIE MACGREGOR
Creator of *Food Duchess*

PAGE STREET
PUBLISHING CO.

PAGE STREET
PUBLISHING CO.

First published in 2021 by

Page Street Publishing Co.

27 Congress Street, Suite 105

Salem, MA 01970

www.pagestreetpublishing.com

Distributed by Macmillan, sales in Canada by The Canadian Manda Group.

25   24   23   22   21   1   2   3   4   5

ISBN-13: 978-1-64567-380-4

ISBN-10: 1-64567-380-4

Library of Congress Control Number: 2021931357

Cover and book design by Rosie Stewart for Page Street Publishing Co.

Photography by Amie MacGregor

Printed and bound in China

Dedication

This book is dedicated to the two most important people in my life. To Sean and my mom, thank you for giving me the continual support and unconditional love that helped me achieve my dreams.

Contents

INTRODUCTION

Baking has always been my passion. My earliest memories involve using my Easy-Bake Oven or helping my mom make cookies in the kitchen. Something about the process was always so soothing and calming for me.

Later in life, baking became not only a huge stress reliever, but my main creative outlet. I never thought of myself as a massively creative person—I can't sing, music was never my thing and I was always terrible in drama class. But baking was a different story. I could not only be creative with all the different combinations and flavors, but the decorating process was always what I considered to be the most creatively rewarding. I loved to watch others revel at the baked masterpiece before them.

From the time I became really seriously passionate about baking—around 15 or 16 years old—I had been told by practically everyone in my life that I should be a baker, open a bakery or do something that involves baking. However, my incredibly analytical and risk-averse mind never thought that my passion for baking could be turned into a sustainable career. As such, I initially chose a career path that was the definition of safe: finance and accounting. After I finished my degree I began working in the field, only to find that I was beyond miserable. I found myself daydreaming about making a living with baking, but I just wasn't quite sure how to start.

I had never even picked up a camera, other than a terrible point-and-shoot or my phone camera, and the whole process of creating a website seemed incredibly daunting to me. After a life-changing conversation with a dear friend of mine, where she convinced me to take a leap of faith, I decided to jump, both feet in, into a whole new world and to follow my dreams. I bought a DSLR camera, watched a million videos online and after a whole lot of trial and error, created a functioning website with some sort of semblance of quality photography on it.

The creation of Food Duchess was initially to satisfy my love for baking, but creating this blog and my online presence helped me find a new passion and creative outlet in my photography.

This book, which brings together my love of over-the-top baking with beautiful, eye-catching photography, has truly been the most rewarding accomplishment of my life. If you're like me and get a massive amount of enjoyment, not only from seeing others enjoy your baked treats, but also from watching them salivate at the name of the cheesecake or watching their eyes pop when they see the beautifully decorated cupcakes in front of them, then this book was made for you.

While a classic brownie can definitely be described as good, a thick fudgy s'mores brownie that sits on top of a crumbly graham cracker base and is crusted with perfectly toasted mini marshmallows is the definition of out-of-this-world good. Throughout this book, you'll find all kinds of these over-the-top fantastic recipes, from richly colored red velvet cinnamon rolls (page 181) to beautifully swirled pumpkin cheesecake bars (page 17). While these desserts and treats can be extravagant, the processes to make them are uncomplicated and can be accomplished by most levels of bakers. It is my true hope that this book fuels your passion for baking, as I know it has done for me!

Annie MacGregor ♡

Irresistible
BARS & BROWNIES

Fudgy. Chewy. Buttery. Ooey-gooey. These are just some of the adjectives that can be used to describe all of the delicious brownies and bars found in this chapter! Each recipe was developed to be sinfully delicious from the get-go. Be it an Impossibly Fudgy S'mores Brownie (page 13) that is decked out with a crunchy graham cracker base and toasted marshmallow topping, or an unbelievably silky pumpkin cheesecake bar (page 17) that will have you saying, "Pumpkin pie who?," this chapter was made for those who love a truly decadent dessert.

IMPOSSIBLY FUDGY S'MORES BROWNIES

All the classic s'mores components come together in this rich, decadent brownie. Graham crackers make up the base of the brownies, laid out evenly on the bottom of the pan to create a simple crust. Thick, fudgy brownie batter is poured over the top, baked and then topped with mini marshmallows and chocolate chips before being placed back under the broiler. The end result is a perfectly golden top, with just a few slightly charred marshmallows, giving that classic smoky, campfire taste to these impossibly delicious s'mores brownies.

MAKES 16 BROWNIES

8 to 10 graham crackers

8 oz (227 g) semisweet chocolate, finely chopped

1½ cups (300 g) white sugar

¾ cup (165 g) packed dark brown sugar

3 large eggs

¾ cup (180 ml) unsalted butter, melted

½ tsp table salt

1 tsp vanilla extract

¾ cup (94 g) all-purpose flour

⅔ cup (60 g) Dutch process cocoa powder

3 cups (150 g) mini marshmallows

¼ cup (42 g) milk chocolate chips

Preheat the oven to 350°F (175°C). Prepare a 9 × 9–inch (23 x 23–cm) baking sheet with cooking spray and place two sheets of parchment in the pan ensuring all sides have been covered. Place the graham crackers in a single layer across the bottom of the prepared sheet (you may need to cut some with a serrated knife to get a perfect fit).

Add the chopped chocolate to a heatproof bowl and place over a pot of simmering water, ensuring the bowl fits tightly over the pot of water and that the bottom of the bowl does not touch the water. Heat, stirring with a rubber spatula, until all of the chocolate has melted. Set aside to cool until just warm (but still very liquid), about 15 minutes.

In a large mixing bowl, combine the white sugar, brown sugar and eggs. Whisk together by hand for about 1 minute. The mixture should look creamy and well combined. Next, pour in the butter, salt, vanilla and melted chocolate. Whisk together until well combined.

Place the flour and cocoa powder into a sieve and sift them into the batter. Fold the sifted flour/cocoa into the batter with a rubber spatula, until the batter is smooth, well combined and thick.

Pour the batter over top of the graham crackers in the prepared pan, then tap it a few times on the counter and place into the oven to bake for 40 to 45 minutes. When done, the brownies will seem slightly jiggly in the center, but they will continue to set as they cool.

Remove the brownies from the oven and place the mini marshmallows in an even layer on top, then sprinkle with chocolate chips. Turn the oven on to broil, and return the pan for about 1 minute to brown the marshmallows. Be sure to keep an eye on the brownies so that the marshmallows don't burn.

Allow the brownies to cool completely in the pan. When ready to serve, use a hot or wet knife to slice the brownies for easier and smoother cutting.

DECADENT BLACK FOREST BROWNIES

Love black forest cake? Then these Decadent Black Forest Brownies are definitely for you!
They are soft, fudgy and brimming with rich chocolate flavor thanks to the real melted
chocolate in the brownie batter. Now, don't forget about the cherries! Cherries make an
appearance throughout the brownies in the form of chopped cherry pieces, kirsch cherry
liqueur, cherry syrup and a literal cherry on top—a maraschino cherry!

MAKES 16 BROWNIES

BLACK FOREST BROWNIES

1 cup (240 ml) canned cherries in syrup

1 cup plus 2 tbsp (140 g) all-purpose flour, divided

10 oz (280 g) semisweet chocolate, finely chopped

2 cups (400 g) white sugar

1 cup (220 g) packed dark brown sugar

4 large eggs

1 cup (240 ml) unsalted butter, melted

1½ tsp (8 ml) vanilla extract

5 tbsp (75 ml) kirsch cherry liqueur

½ cup (38 g) Dutch process cocoa powder, sifted

½ tsp table salt

BLACK FOREST BROWNIES

Preheat the oven to 350°F (175°C). Prepare a 9 × 9–inch (23 x 23–cm) baking sheet with cooking spray and parchment.

Drain the syrup from the cherries, reserving ½ cup (120 ml) of the syrup. Set the syrup aside for later. Measure out the cherries, then roughly chop them. Sprinkle the 2 tablespoons (16 g) of flour over the chopped cherries, toss to coat and set aside.

Add the chopped chocolate to a heatproof bowl and place it over a pot of simmering water, ensuring the bowl fits tightly over the pot of water and that the bottom does not touch the water. Heat, stirring with a rubber spatula, until all of the chocolate has melted. Set aside to cool until just warm while you continue on.

In a large mixing bowl, combine the white sugar, brown sugar and eggs. Whisk together by hand for about 1 minute. The mixture should look creamy and well combined. Next, pour in the melted butter, vanilla, kirsch and melted chocolate. Whisk together until well combined.

In a separate bowl, whisk together the remaining 1 cup (125 g) of flour, sifted cocoa powder and salt. Add these dry ingredients into the wet ingredients, then fold them into the batter with a rubber spatula until the batter is smooth, well combined and thick. Add in the dredged cherries and fold them in.

Pour the batter into the prepared pan and smooth it out. Place into the oven to bake for 40 to 45 minutes. When done, the brownies will seem slightly underbaked in the center, but they will continue to set as they cool.

(continued)

CHERRY SYRUP

½ cup (120 ml) reserved canned cherry syrup

¼ cup (60 ml) kirsch cherry liqueur

TOPPING

1 cup (240 ml) heavy cream, chilled

1 tbsp (8 g) confectioners' sugar

16 maraschino cherries

CHERRY SYRUP

Add the reserved cherry syrup and the kirsch to a small saucepan over medium heat. Bring to a boil, then simmer for 10 to 15 minutes, or until reduced by half.

Remove the syrup from the stove, then brush six to seven times over the top of the brownies. Allow the brownies to absorb the syrup and cool completely before slicing and serving.

TOPPING

In the bowl of a stand mixer fitted with the whisk attachment, combine the heavy cream and confectioners' sugar. Beat the cream on medium-high speed until stiff peaks have formed.

Slice the brownies into 16 servings, then top each brownie with a dollop or piping of the whipped cream, then place a cherry on top of each. Keep cold or serve immediately.

NOT-SO-BASIC PUMPKIN PIE CHEESECAKE BARS

My mom, as a lifelong cheesecake lover, is my official cheesecake taster. When I gave her these to try, she practically ate the whole pan in a day—yes, they're THAT good. Not only are they gorgeous, with their swirly marble pattern, but the flavor is unmatched! They're rich and creamy, as cheesecake should be, with that nostalgic pumpkin pie spice that everyone loves.

MAKES 20 BARS

GRAHAM CRACKER CRUST

2¼ cups (300 g) graham cracker crumbs

⅓ cup (66 g) white sugar

10 tbsp (150 ml) unsalted butter, melted

PUMPKIN CHEESECAKE

4 (8-oz [227-g]) blocks cream cheese, well softened

1½ cups (300 g) white sugar

1 tbsp (15 ml) vanilla extract

¼ tsp table salt

3 large eggs, at room temperature

2 large egg yolks, at room temperature

¾ cup (180 ml) heavy cream

1 tbsp (8 g) cornstarch

¾ cup (184 g) pumpkin purée

2 tsp (5 g) cinnamon

1 tsp allspice

½ tsp ground ginger

⅛ tsp nutmeg

6 tbsp (90 ml) sour cream

GRAHAM CRACKER CRUST

Preheat the oven to 350°F (175°C). In a large bowl, combine the graham cracker crumbs and sugar and whisk well. Pour the melted butter into the bowl, then mix with a fork, or your hands, until the butter is well dispersed and the mixture resembles wet sand.

Grease a 9 x 13–inch (23 x 33–cm) baking sheet and add two pieces of parchment to cover all sides of the pan. Pour the crust into the pan and press it down evenly into the bottom. Use a flat-bottomed measuring cup to really compact it. Put the crust into the oven to bake for 10 minutes. Remove the crust from the oven and allow it to cool to room temperature.

PUMPKIN CHEESECAKE

Turn the oven down to 325°F (160°C). In a large mixing bowl or the bowl of a stand mixer, place the softened cream cheese and beat on low until it looks soft and creamy, about 2 minutes. Add the sugar, vanilla and salt, and beat on low until very creamy, 3 to 4 minutes. While still beating on low, add the eggs and yolks, one at a time, ensuring that each egg is fully incorporated before adding the next, scraping down the sides of the bowl as necessary. Add the heavy cream and cornstarch, then beat on low until the cheesecake filling looks creamy, smooth and uniform.

Divide the batter into two bowls. In one bowl add the pumpkin purée, cinnamon, allspice, ginger and nutmeg, then beat until smooth. In the other bowl, put the sour cream and then beat until smooth.

(continued)

Spoon each batter, alternating each time, over the top of the cooled graham cracker crust. After all of the batter from both bowls has been added, use a wooden skewer or a knife to swirl the batters together in the pan.

Place into the oven to bake for 40 to 45 minutes. When the cheesecake is done it should still be a little jiggly in the center.

When done, lightly crack the oven open to allow the cheesecake to slowly cool in the oven for about 1½ hours. After an hour, remove the cheesecake from the oven and place onto the counter to cool to room temperature. Once at room temperature, wrap the cheesecake with plastic wrap and place it into the fridge for at least 6 hours or preferably overnight.

CHEWY BIRTHDAY CAKE BLONDIES

These birthday cake–inspired blondies are like the love child of funfetti birthday cake and tender golden cookies! Chewy, sweet and full of rainbow sprinkle fun—these blondies are out-of-this-world good. The vanilla and rainbow sprinkles bring that classic birthday cake flavor to the party, and the bread flour, thanks to its higher gluten content, makes these blondies irresistibly chewy in texture.

MAKES 16 BARS

1⅓ cups (165 g) all-purpose flour

1 cup (137 g) bread flour

1 tsp baking powder

¾ tsp table salt

1 cup (240 ml) unsalted butter, melted

1 cup (220 g) packed light brown sugar

¾ cup (150 g) white sugar

2 large eggs

1 tbsp (15 ml) vanilla extract

¾ cup (126 g) white chocolate chips

¾ cup (150 g) sprinkles

Preheat the oven to 350°F (175°C). Prepare a 9 × 9–inch (23 x 23–cm) baking sheet with cooking spray and parchment.

In a medium- to large-sized bowl, combine the all-purpose flour, bread flour, baking powder and salt. Whisk well, then set aside.

In a large mixing bowl, put the melted butter, brown sugar and white sugar and beat with a hand mixer until combined.

Add the eggs and vanilla, then beat until well combined, scraping at the edges periodically. Add in the flour mixture and mix on low until combined, scraping down the edges. Ensure it is well combined, but do not overmix. Add in the white chocolate and sprinkles, then fold with a spatula until well dispersed.

Transfer the blondie batter to the prepared baking sheet and smooth it out evenly. Place into the oven to bake for 30 to 35 minutes, or until the center barely wobbles when shaken. Allow to cool completely before slicing.

CRUMBLY APPLE PIE BARS

While I love pumpkin, my first love has always been apple. Apple pie, apple crisp or apple cake—I love it all. These apple pie crumble bars taste just like a cross between apple pie and apple crisp, but in a small, handheld package! What more could you ask for?

MAKES 16 BARS

SHORTBREAD CRUST

⅔ cup (150 g) unsalted butter, at room temperature

½ cup (100 g) white sugar

¾ tsp vanilla extract

1½ cups (185 g) all-purpose flour

APPLE PIE FILLING

4 medium apples, peeled and diced (see Note)

¼ cup (55 g) packed dark brown sugar

2 tbsp (16 g) cornstarch

1 tsp vanilla extract

¾ tsp lemon juice

1 tsp cinnamon

½ tsp ground ginger

Pinch nutmeg

Pinch table salt

CRUMBLE TOPPING

¾ cup (68 g) rolled oats

¾ cup (94 g) all-purpose flour

¾ cup (165 g) packed light brown sugar (dark can also be used)

¾ tsp cinnamon

½ tsp baking powder

Pinch table salt

6 tbsp (90 ml) unsalted butter, melted

SHORTBREAD CRUST

Preheat the oven to 350°F (175°C) and prepare a 9 × 9–inch (23 x 23–cm) baking sheet with cooking spray and parchment.

In a mixing bowl, combine the butter, sugar and vanilla, then beat with a hand mixer until smooth. Add in the flour, then beat again until a crumbly dough comes together.

Pour the dough into the pan and press it down evenly into the bottom. Place into the oven to bake for 18 minutes. Remove the crust from the oven, press down any puffed-up parts, then allow to cool to room temperature.

APPLE PIE FILLING

Put all of the apple pie filling ingredients together in a mixing bowl, then toss together until everything is well dispersed. Pour the apple pie filling over the top of the cooled shortbread crust, then press down to even everything out.

CRUMBLE TOPPING

In a medium mixing bowl, combine the oats, flour, brown sugar, cinnamon, baking powder and salt. Whisk together to combine. Pour in the melted butter and toss with a fork or mix with your hands until the butter is well dispersed and evenly coats everything.

Sprinkle the crumble topping evenly over the apple filling, press down lightly, then place into the oven to bake for 50 minutes. When done, the top should feel crisp and be golden in color. Remove the bars from the oven, allow to cool completely, then slice into 16 squares.

Note: *These apple pie crumble bars are best with a sweet-tart variety of apple that can hold its shape during baking. Look for varieties such as Pink Lady (my personal choice), Braeburn or even Honeycrisp (which is a touch more sweet).*

THICK AND FUDGY ROCKY ROAD BROWNIE SKILLET

This is truly like magic in a pan. These ultra-decadent chocolate brownies are scattered with fluffy mini marshmallows and crunchy whole peanuts, and swirled with everyone's favorite—peanut butter! This skillet brownie is excellent by itself, but I highly recommend you eat it while it's warm with a little vanilla ice cream on top.

MAKES 1 (9-INCH (23-CM)) BROWNIE SKILLET

6 oz (170 g) semisweet chocolate, finely chopped

1½ cups (300 g) white sugar

¾ cup (165 g) packed dark brown sugar

3 large eggs

¾ cup (180 ml) unsalted butter, melted

1½ tsp (7.5 ml) vanilla extract

1 cup (125 g) all-purpose flour

¾ cup (56 g) Dutch process cocoa powder, sifted

½ tsp table salt

1 cup (240 ml) creamy natural peanut butter, divided

¾ cup (38 g) mini marshmallows, divided

¾ cup (110 g) peanuts, divided

Preheat the oven to 350°F (175°C). Prepare a 9-inch (23-cm) oven-safe skillet with cooking spray.

Put the chopped chocolate in a heatproof bowl and place it over a pot of simmering water, ensuring the bowl fits tightly over the pot and that the bottom does not touch the water. Heat, while stirring with a rubber spatula, until all of the chocolate has melted. Set aside to cool until just warm while you continue on.

In a large mixing bowl, combine the white sugar, brown sugar and eggs. Whisk together by hand for about 1 minute. The mixture should look creamy and well combined. Next, pour in the melted butter, vanilla and melted chocolate. Whisk together until well combined.

In a separate bowl, whisk together the flour, sifted cocoa powder and salt. Add these dry ingredients into the wet ingredients, then mix them into the batter with a rubber spatula, until the batter is smooth, well combined and thick. Add in half of the peanut butter, half of the marshmallows and half of the peanuts, then lightly fold to incorporate.

Pour the batter into the prepared skillet and smooth it out. Dollop the remaining peanut butter on top, then swirl it in with a knife or wood skewer and sprinkle with the remaining peanuts. Place into the oven to bake for 45 minutes.

Remove the brownie from the oven and sprinkle with the remaining marshmallows. Place the brownie under the broiler, and broil for 1 to 2 minutes—just until the marshmallows begin to turn golden. Allow the brownie skillet to cool and firm up for about 30 minutes before consuming. Enjoy warm with ice cream.

Killer
COOKIES & MACARONS

Macarons, cookie sandwiches and stuffed cookies are just some of the recipes you'll find on these next pages. These treats are not made for those with just a delicate sweet tooth. No, this chapter is dedicated to those who are categorically and unequivocally cookie-obsessed! From red velvet cookies stuffed with velvety cream cheese frosting (page 34) to s'mores macarons (page 45) that are sandwiched with toasted marshmallow and dipped in chocolate, these recipes will definitely satisfy your little cookie-loving heart!

BUTTERY APPLE PIE LINZER COOKIES

As a child, my favorite dessert was apple pie. There is nothing quite like the warm, cozy flavor of cinnamon mixed with apples. I looked forward to it every year around the holidays. Well, with Apple Pie Linzer Cookies there is no need to wait all year to enjoy that nostalgic taste. These are quite simple to make and just as delicious as a good ol' slice of apple pie!

MAKES 12 SANDWICH COOKIES

APPLE PIE FILLING
¼ cup (60 ml) apple jelly, cold
½ tsp cinnamon
⅛ tsp vanilla extract
Pinch table salt

LINZER COOKIES
¾ cup (71 g) almond flour
1⅓ cups (165 g) all-purpose flour, plus more for dusting
¼ tsp table salt
¾ cup (170 g) unsalted butter, at room temperature
½ cup (100 g) white sugar
1½ tsp (4 g) cinnamon
1 large egg yolk
1 tsp vanilla extract
2 tbsp (16 g) confectioners' sugar, for dusting

APPLE PIE FILLING
Put the apple jelly, cinnamon, vanilla and salt in a small mixing bowl. Whisk or stir together until smooth. Set aside for later.

LINZER COOKIES
Preheat the oven to 350°F (175°C) and prepare two baking sheets with parchment. Evenly spread the almond flour onto one baking sheet, then place into the oven to toast. Bake for about 15 minutes, ensuring that you stir the mixture every 5 minutes to promote even toasting. Remove the toasted almond flour from the oven and allow it to cool for about 30 minutes.

In a medium mixing bowl, whisk together the cooled almond flour, all-purpose flour and salt. Set aside.

In a stand mixer fitted with the paddle attachment, beat together the butter, sugar and cinnamon until light and fluffy, 3 to 5 minutes. Add the egg yolk and vanilla, then beat again until well combined. Add the flour mixture to the stand mixer and beat until just combined and a crumbly-looking dough has formed.

Remove the dough from the stand mixer and lightly form into a disk shape with your hands. Place the dough disk onto a heavily floured surface, and roll the dough out to ⅛ to ¼ inch (3 to 6 mm) thick. Using a 2½-inch (6-cm) round cookie cutter, cut out the cookies. Carefully place the cookies onto the baking sheet (I find it's easiest to use a metal spatula to lift them off the counter).

Using a mini cookie cutter or the back of a piping tip (for a round shape), cut out the center of half of the cookies. Place both baking sheets into the freezer for 15 minutes. After the 15 minutes, place the cookies into the oven to bake for 10 minutes. Allow them to cool before filling. When cooled, dust the cookies with the centers cut out with confectioners' sugar, and spread 1 teaspoon of apple pie filling onto the remaining cookies. Sandwich the two halves together.

RAINBOW-SPECKLED BIRTHDAY CAKE SHORTBREAD COOKIES

Who doesn't love a classic shortbread cookie with its sweet, sugary taste and unbelievably buttery texture? These birthday cake shortbread cookies utilize lots of vanilla and heaps of colorful sprinkles to turn classic shortbread into birthday cake shortbread!

MAKES 18 TO 20 COOKIES

BIRTHDAY CAKE SHORTBREAD COOKIES

2 cups (454 g) unsalted butter, at room temperature

1 cup (200 g) white sugar

2 tsp (10 ml) vanilla extract

½ tsp table salt

4 cups (500 g) all-purpose flour

¼ cup (50 g) round (nonpareils) sprinkles

GLAZE

2 cups (240 g) confectioners' sugar

10 tbsp (150 ml) heavy cream

Sprinkles, for decorating

BIRTHDAY CAKE SHORTBREAD COOKIES

Prepare two baking sheets with parchment. In a mixing bowl, combine the butter, sugar, vanilla and salt, then beat with a hand mixer until smooth. Add in the flour, then beat again until a crumbly dough comes together. Finally, add in the sprinkles and quickly beat again to distribute.

Form the crumbly dough into a disk or ball with your hands, then place onto a floured surface. Roll the dough out to be about ¼ inch (6 mm) thick. Cut round cookies out of the dough using a 2½-inch (6-cm) round cookie cutter. Using a thin metal spatula, transfer each cookie onto the prepared cookie sheets. Place into the freezer for 15 minutes.

Meanwhile, preheat the oven to 325°F (160°C). Place the cookies into the oven to bake for 10 to 15 minutes, or until the edges just begin to turn golden. Allow the cookies to cool completely before glazing.

GLAZE

In a mixing bowl, combine that confectioners' sugar and cream, then whisk together until smooth. Dip half of each cooled cookie into the glaze, then immediately top with sprinkles. Allow the glaze to set before enjoying.

Note: If your cookies spread slightly, use the cookie cutter to recut them while they're still hot to achieve perfectly round cookies.

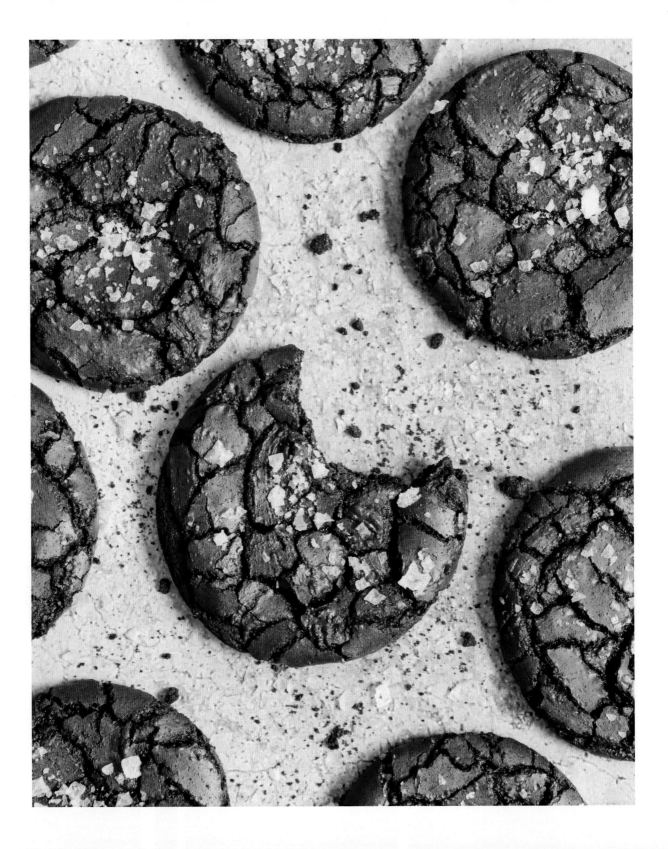

CRINKLY BROWNIE COOKIES

These brownie cookies can only be described in one way: sinfully delicious. Seriously!
They're out-of-this-world fudgy, and have a crinkly, crispy exterior—making them
a dead ringer for a brownie but, you know, in cookie form!

MAKES 12 COOKIES

7 oz (198 g) semisweet chocolate, finely chopped

½ cup (114 g) unsalted butter, at room temperature

¾ cup (165 g) packed dark brown sugar

½ cup (100 g) white sugar

2 large eggs

1 tsp vanilla extract

1 cup plus 2 tsp (136 g) all-purpose flour

3 tbsp (15 g) black cocoa powder (double-Dutch) or Dutch process cocoa powder

1 tsp baking powder

½ tsp table salt

Flaky salt, for garnish

Preheat the oven to 350°F (175°C) and prepare two baking sheets with parchment paper. Put the chopped chocolate and butter into a heat-proof bowl and place over the top of a simmering pot of water. Ensure the bottom of the bowl isn't touching the water. Heat and stir until all of the chocolate and butter is melted. Allow it to cool slightly while you begin making the cookies.

In the bowl of a stand mixer fitted with a paddle attachment, combine the brown sugar, white sugar, eggs and vanilla, then beat until the mixture looks fluffy and has almost tripled in volume—3 to 4 minutes on high. Add the slightly cooled melted chocolate mixture to the stand mixer, then mix until well combined with the rest of the batter.

In a separate bowl, combine the flour, cocoa powder, baking powder and table salt, then whisk until well combined. Then add this mixture to the stand mixer and beat on medium-low until just combined and smooth.

Using a 1½-ounce (45-ml) cookie scoop, scoop the batter onto the two baking sheets (each sheet gets six cookies). The batter will be very thick and viscous—similar to brownie batter. It is best to work fast because the batter becomes hard to work with once it begins to cool.

Sprinkle the cookies with a little bit of flaky salt, then bake the cookies, one sheet at a time, for 12 minutes each. Allow the cookies to cool completely before enjoying.

STUFFED RED VELVET COOKIES

Stuffed Red Velvet Cookies. Need I say more? A rich cocoa-infused cookie dough is wrapped around sweet little balls of cream cheese frosting and baked to make a tender, chewy red velvet cookie with an oozy center.

MAKES 16 TO 18 COOKIES

CREAM CHEESE FILLING

1¾ cups (210 g) confectioners' sugar

½ cup (116 g) softened cream cheese

1 tbsp (8 g) all-purpose flour

½ tsp vanilla extract

RED VELVET COOKIES

2½ cups (315 g) all-purpose flour

¼ cup (22 g) cocoa powder, sifted

1 tsp table salt

¾ tsp baking powder

¾ tsp baking soda

1 cup (227 g) unsalted butter, at room temperature

1 cup (220 g) packed dark brown sugar

½ cup (100 g) white sugar

2 large eggs

1 tbsp (15 ml) red gel food coloring

1 tsp vanilla extract

1 cup (168 g) white chocolate chips

Note: *If working in batches, keep uncooked cookies in the fridge or freezer until you bake them.*

CREAM CHEESE FILLING

In a large mixing bowl, combine all of the cream cheese filling ingredients and beat together until smooth. Using a spoon, scoop out 2-teaspoon (10-ml) sized dollops onto a baking sheet fitted with parchment paper. Place into the freezer for at least 2 hours.

After 2 hours, remove the filling from the freezer. Working very quickly, roll the dollops into a ball shape with your hands. If they are too soft to roll, return to the freezer for another hour. After all have been shaped, return to the freezer for at least another 2 hours, or preferably longer.

RED VELVET COOKIES

In a medium- to large-sized bowl, combine the flour, sifted cocoa powder, salt, baking powder and baking soda. Whisk well, then set aside.

In the bowl of a stand mixer fitted with the paddle attachment, combine the butter, brown sugar and white sugar and beat for 3 minutes, until light, fluffy and doubled in volume. In a separate bowl, whisk together the eggs, red food coloring and vanilla, then add to the sugar and butter mixture and beat on high for another 2 minutes, scraping down the edges periodically. Add in the flour mixture and mix on low until well combined, scraping the edges. Do not overmix. Add in the white chocolate chips, then fold in with a spatula.

Using a 1½-ounce (45-ml) cookie scoop, scoop out the cookie dough. Take a scoop of dough into your hands, then flatten it between your palms. Place a frozen cream cheese frosting ball into the center of the cookie, then wrap the overhanging around the ball, ensuring that it's fully encased and sealed. Transfer the cookie to the freezer. Repeat with the remaining cookie dough and cream cheese balls. Freeze all of the cookies for 15 minutes.

Meanwhile, preheat the oven to 350°F (175°C) and prepare three baking sheets with parchment paper. Place the cookies onto baking sheets (six per sheet), then place into the oven to bake for 13 minutes. Allow the cookies to cool for at least half an hour before enjoying.

DREAMY CRÈME BRÛLÉE MACARONS

The most popular recipes on my website for years now have always been my macaron recipes! This book would, therefore, not be complete without a few truly decadent and fabulous macaron recipes! This first macaron recipe is inspired by a classic OG dessert—crème brûlée. It features classic macaron shells that are filled with a vanilla custard–infused buttercream, and then topped with sugar that is brûléed to burnt delicious perfection! *Note: As macarons can be quite finicky and sensitive to variances in the measurements, I highly recommend that you use a kitchen scale and measure the macaron ingredients using the weight (grams) given, rather than going by volume.*

MAKES 18 MACARONS

VANILLA CUSTARD BUTTERCREAM

1 large egg

2½ tbsp (37 ml) heavy cream

2½ tbsp (37 g) white sugar

½ cup (114 g) plus 1 tbsp (14 g) unsalted butter, at room temperature, divided

1 tsp vanilla extract

Pinch table salt

¼ cup (30 g) confectioners' sugar

MACARONS

105 g (1 cup plus 1½ tbsp) superfine almond flour

105 g (14 tbsp) confectioners' sugar

100 g (6 tbsp plus 2 tsp) fresh egg whites

100 g (½ cup) white sugar

3 g (1 tsp) egg white powder, otherwise known as meringue powder (optional but highly recommended)

¼ cup (48 g) superfine sugar (for burnt sugar topping)

VANILLA CUSTARD BUTTERCREAM

In a medium metal bowl, combine the egg, heavy cream and white sugar and whisk together. Set the bowl over the top of a simmering pot of water, making sure that a tight seal forms and that the bottom of the bowl is not actually touching the water.

Continuously whisk the mixture while it heats up over the simmering water, heating the mixture just until it begins to bubble and thickens slightly. Remove from the heat, add in the 1 tablespoon (14 g) of butter, vanilla and salt, then whisk until combined. Transfer into another bowl, then place a piece of plastic wrap on the surface of the custard and place it into the fridge to cool for at least 4 hours, or overnight.

MACARONS: DRY INGREDIENTS

Prepare a baking sheet with parchment or a silicone mat (if you have enough, prepare two baking sheets).

Over a large mixing bowl on a scale, sift the almond flour until you reach 105 grams. Discard any large pieces of almond flour. Repeat with the confectioners' sugar. Whisk the almond flour and confectioners' sugar until very well combined. Set aside.

(continued)

DREAMY CRÈME BRÛLÉE MACARONS (CONTINUED)

MAKING THE MERINGUE

In the bowl of a stand mixer, combine the egg whites, white sugar and egg white powder and whisk together by hand until just combined. Set the bowl over the simmering water, making sure a tight seal forms and that the bottom of the stand mixer bowl is not actually touching the water.

Continuously whisk the mixture by hand while it heats up over the simmering water, heating the mixture until it reaches 140°F (60°C) on a kitchen thermometer. When this temperature is achieved, remove the bowl from the simmering water pot and place it onto your stand mixer, fitted with the whisk attachment.

Beat the mixture, starting on low. Once soft peaks have formed, increase the speed to medium. Once medium peaks are achieved, increase the speed to high. Beat on high until stiff peaks have formed. You can mostly judge by appearance, but each iteration takes roughly 2 to 3 minutes.

MACARONAGE

Remove the bowl from the stand mixer, and place a sieve over the top. Pour the dry mixture from earlier into the sieve, then sift the dry ingredients into the meringue.

Fold the dry ingredients into the meringue. I like to scrape around the sides of the bowl in an entire circle, and then cut through the center.

Be gentle and careful not to overmix or overdeflate the meringue. The mixture is ready to be piped when it ribbons off your spatula, meaning that the batter, when lifted with a spatula, should keep flowing off the spatula in ribbon shapes nonstop, without drizzling off too quickly. If it is coming off in large V-shaped chunks, it still needs to be folded further. Another test is the figure-8 test: If you can lift some batter up and use it to draw several figure 8s without the stream breaking, it is ready!

PIPING AND DRYING THE MACARONS

Add the mixture to a piping bag with a medium- to large-sized round tip. Pipe small circles of batter onto a cookie sheet fitted with a silicone baking mat or parchment paper. Ensure the piping bag is held straight up and perpendicular to the baking sheet. Using a stencil or a macaron mat makes this process much easier and foolproof; I try to make my macarons about 1½ inches (4 cm) in diameter.

Tap the baking sheet multiple times against the counter to remove any air bubbles from the macarons. If some air bubbles still remain, use a toothpick to gently poke them out.

Preheat the oven to 300°F (150°C), or 275°F (135°C) for a convection oven. While the oven is preheating, allow the macarons to sit and form a skin. This skin will ensure the macarons bake up and not out, giving them those classic "feet." This skin should form anywhere from 8 minutes to an hour. You know the macarons are ready to be baked when you can touch them lightly without having the batter stick to your finger. Keep checking them to see if they have formed a skin—overly dried macarons are just as much of a problem as under dried ones!

BAKING

Bake for 15 to 20 minutes. Your bake time will depend on the size of your macarons. The macarons are ready when the tops are firm and do not move around their base at all. Check at 15 minutes, and if they are not ready then keep checking every minute.

Allow the macarons to cool completely before attempting to remove. When cooled, find perfect pairs of macaron halves and set them aside to be filled and topped.

FINISHING THE VANILLA CUSTARD BUTTERCREAM

When the custard is cooled, place the ½ cup (120 ml) of butter into a stand mixer fitted with the whisk attachment. Whip the butter on high for 5 minutes. When done, the butter should look fluffy and white. Add the vanilla custard into the stand mixer in three additions, ensuring that you beat well after each addition to fully incorporate the custard.

After all of the custard has been incorporated, add in the confectioners' sugar and beat again until well combined and fluffy.

FILLING AND ASSEMBLY

Put the buttercream into a piping bag fitted with a star tip, then pipe onto half of the macaron shells (the bottoms of each perfect pair), then top each bottom with its corresponding top. Place into the fridge overnight to mature and meld together.

The next day, lightly brush the top of each macaron with water, then dip the wet top into the superfine sugar. Carefully use a kitchen torch to brûlée the sugar.

"CHRISTMAS IN A COOKIE"
GINGERBREAD MACARONS

While gingerbread is an absolute must during the holiday season, who says it can't be enjoyed any time of year? These cinnamon-, allspice- and ginger-spiced macaron shells, when paired with velvety molasses buttercream, give that classic gingerbread flavor but in a fancier, petite little macaron package! *Note: As macarons can be quite finicky and sensitive to variances in the measurements, I highly recommend that you use a kitchen scale and measure the macaron ingredients using the weight (grams) given, rather than going by volume.*

MAKES 18 MACARONS

MACARONS

105 g (1 cup plus 1½ tbsp) superfine almond flour

105 g (14 tbsp) confectioners' sugar

100 g (6 tbsp plus 2 tsp) fresh egg whites

100 g (½ cup) white sugar

3 g (1 tsp) egg white powder, otherwise known as meringue powder (optional but highly recommended)

Brown gel food coloring (optional)

1 tsp cinnamon

½ tsp ground ginger

½ tsp allspice

DRY INGREDIENTS

Prepare a baking sheet with parchment or a silicone mat (if you have enough, prepare two baking sheets).

Over a large mixing bowl on a scale, sift the almond flour until you reach 105 grams. Discard any large pieces of almond flour. Repeat with the confectioners' sugar. Whisk the almond flour and confectioners' sugar until well combined. Set aside.

MAKING THE MERINGUE

In the bowl of your stand mixer, combine the egg whites, white sugar and egg white powder and whisk together. Set the bowl over the top of a simmering pot of water, making sure a tight seal forms and that the bottom of the stand mixer bowl is not actually touching the water.

Continuously whisk the mixture by hand while it heats up over the simmering water, heating the mixture until it reaches 140°F (60°C) on a kitchen thermometer. When this temperature is reached, remove the bowl from the simmering water pot and place onto your stand mixer, fitted with the whisk attachment.

Beat the mixture, starting on low. Once soft peaks form, increase the speed to medium. Once medium peaks are achieved, increase the speed to high. Beat on high until stiff peaks form. You can mostly judge by appearance, but each iteration takes roughly 2 to 3 minutes. Add in the brown food coloring (if using), and beat again for 30 seconds to fully incorporate.

(continued)

"CHRISTMAS IN A COOKIE" GINGERBREAD MACARONS (CONTINUED)

MACARONAGE

Remove the bowl from the stand mixer, and place a sieve over the top. Pour the dry mixture from earlier into the sieve, then sift the dry ingredients into the meringue.

Fold the dry ingredients into the meringue. I like to scrape around the sides of the bowl in an entire circle, and then cut through the center.

When the batter is about halfway folded to the proper consistency (read more on that below), sift in the cinnamon, ginger and allspice. Fold the spices in while you continue to fold the batter.

Be gentle and careful not to overmix or overdeflate the meringue. The mixture is ready to be piped when it ribbons off your spatula, meaning that the batter, when lifted with a spatula, should keep flowing off the spatula in ribbon shapes nonstop, without drizzling off too quickly. If it is coming off in large V-shaped chunks, it still needs to be folded further. Another test is the figure-8 test: If you can lift some batter up and use it to draw several figure 8s without the stream breaking, it is ready!

PIPING AND DRYING THE MACARONS

Put the mixture into a piping bag with a medium- to large-sized round tip. Pipe small circles of batter onto a cookie sheet fitted with a silicone baking mat or parchment paper. Ensure that the piping bag is held straight up and perpendicular to the baking sheet. Using a stencil or a macaron mat makes this process much easier and foolproof; I try to make my macarons about 1½ inches (4 cm) in diameter.

Tap the baking sheet multiple times against the counter to remove any air bubbles from the macarons. If some air bubbles still remain, use a toothpick to gently poke them out.

Preheat the oven to 300°F (150°C), or 275°F (135°C) for a convection oven. While the oven is preheating, allow the macarons to sit and form a skin. This skin will ensure the macarons bake up and not out, giving them those classic "feet." This skin should form anywhere from 8 minutes to an hour. You know the macarons are ready to be baked when you can touch them lightly without having the batter stick to your finger. Keep checking them to see if they have formed a skin—overly dried macarons are just as much of a problem as under dried ones!

MOLASSES BUTTERCREAM

½ cup (114 g) unsalted butter, at room temperature

1¾ cups (210 g) confectioners' sugar

1 tbsp (15 ml) fancy molasses

1 tsp (5 ml) vanilla extract

BAKING

Bake for 15 to 20 minutes. Your bake time will depend on the size of your macarons. The macarons are ready when the tops are firm and do not move around their base at all. Check at 15 minutes, and if they are not ready then keep checking every minute.

Allow the macarons to cool completely before attempting to remove them. When cooled, find perfect pairs of macaron halves and set them aside to be filled.

MOLASSES BUTTERCREAM

Add the butter to a stand mixer fitted with the whisk attachment. Beat on high until the butter is doubled in volume and looks light and fluffy.

Turn the stand mixer to low and slowly add the confectioners' sugar. Beat until completely incorporated, then add in the molasses and vanilla. Beat until well combined and fully incorporated.

FILLING AND ASSEMBLY

Put the molasses buttercream in a piping bag fitted with a round tip, then pipe the buttercream onto half of the macaron shells (the bottoms of each perfect pair), then top each bottom with its corresponding top. Place the cookies into the fridge overnight to mature and meld together.

SMOKY S'MORES MACARONS

Ditch the campfire and sticks, because these s'mores macarons have got your s'mores craving covered! These delicate, yet mighty delicious, chocolate macarons have a center made of glossy ganache and fluffy torched marshmallow, and are dipped in melted dark chocolate and sprinkled with graham cracker crumbs! *Note: As macarons can be quite finicky and sensitive to variances in the measurements, I highly recommend that you use a kitchen scale and measure the macaron ingredients using the weight (grams) given, rather than going by volume.*

MAKES 18 MACARONS

MILK CHOCOLATE GANACHE
6 tbsp (90 ml) heavy cream

4.3 oz (120 g) milk chocolate, finely chopped

CHOCOLATE MACARONS
98 g (1 cup) superfine almond flour

97 g (13 tbsp) confectioners' sugar

15 g (3 tbsp) cocoa powder, preferably Dutch process

100 g (6 tbsp plus 2 tsp) fresh egg whites

100 g (½ cup) white sugar

3 g (1 tsp) egg white powder, otherwise known as meringue powder (optional but highly recommended)

Brown gel food coloring (optional)

MILK CHOCOLATE GANACHE

In a medium saucepan over medium heat, pour the cream. Heat until it begins to simmer.

Put the chopped chocolate in a heatproof medium mixing bowl, then pour the hot cream over it. Stir lightly with a spatula, then let the mixture sit for 3 minutes to melt the chocolate. After 3 minutes, whisk the ganache until the cream and chocolate are incorporated together and smooth.

Cover the ganache with plastic wrap, then place it in the fridge to cool for at least 3 to 4 hours, or preferably overnight.

MACARONS: DRY INGREDIENTS

Prepare a baking sheet with parchment or a silicone mat (if you have enough, prepare two baking sheets).

Over a large mixing bowl on a scale, sift the almond flour until you reach 98 grams. Discard any large pieces of almond flour. Repeat with the confectioners' sugar and cocoa powder. Whisk the almond flour, confectioners' sugar and cocoa together until very well combined. Set aside.

(continued)

MAKING THE MERINGUE

In the bowl of a stand mixer, combine the egg whites, white sugar and egg white powder and whisk together. Set the bowl over the top of a simmering pot of water, making sure a tight seal forms and that the bottom of the stand mixer bowl is not actually touching the water.

Continuously whisk the mixture by hand while it heats up over the simmering water, heating until it reaches 140°F (60°C) on a kitchen thermometer. When this temperature is reached, remove the bowl from the simmering water pot and place it onto your stand mixer, fitted with the whisk attachment.

Beat the mixture, starting on low. Once soft peaks form, increase the speed to medium. Once medium peaks are achieved, increase the speed to high. Beat on high until stiff peaks form. You can mostly judge by appearance, but each iteration takes roughly 2 to 3 minutes. Add in the brown food coloring (if using), and beat again for 30 seconds to fully incorporate.

MACARONAGE

Remove the bowl from the stand mixer and place a sieve over the top. Pour the dry mixture from earlier into the sieve, then sift the dry ingredients into the meringue.

Fold the dry ingredients into the meringue. I like to scrape around the sides of the bowl in a circle, and then cut through the center.

Be gentle and careful not to overmix or overdeflate the meringue. The mixture is ready to be piped when it ribbons off your spatula, meaning that the batter, when lifted with a spatula, should keep flowing off the spatula in ribbon shapes nonstop, without drizzling off too quickly. If it is coming off in large V-shaped chunks it still needs to be folded further. Another test is the figure-8 test: If you can lift some batter up and use it to draw several figure 8s without the stream breaking, it is ready!

PIPING AND DRYING THE MACARONS

Put the mixture in a piping bag with a medium- to large-sized round tip. Pipe small circles of batter onto the prepared baking sheet. Ensure the piping bag is held straight up and down, perpendicular to the baking sheet. Using a stencil or a macaron mat makes this process much easier and foolproof; I try to make my macarons about 1½ inches (4 cm) in diameter.

Tap the baking sheet multiple times against the counter to remove any air bubbles from the macarons. If some air bubbles still remain, use a toothpick to gently poke them out.

Preheat the oven to 300°F (150°C), or 275°F (135°C) for a convection oven. While the oven is preheating, allow the macarons to sit and form a skin. This skin will ensure the macarons bake up and not out, giving them those classic "feet." This skin should form anywhere from 8 minutes to an hour. You know the macarons are ready to be baked when you can touch them lightly without having the batter stick to your finger. Keep checking them to see if they have formed a skin—overly dried macarons are just as much of a problem as under dried macarons!

MARSHMALLOW FILLING

¼ cup plus 1 tsp (65 g) fresh egg whites

½ cup (100 g) white sugar

1 tsp vanilla extract

TOPPING AND ASSEMBLY

4 oz (113 g) semisweet chocolate, melted and cooled to room temperature

2 tbsp (16 g) graham cracker crumbs

BAKING

Bake for 15 to 25 minutes. Your bake time will depend on the size of your macarons. The macarons are ready when the tops are firm and do not move around their base at all. Check at 15 minutes, and if they are not ready then keep checking every minute.

Allow the macarons to cool completely before attempting to remove them. When cooled, find perfect pairs of macaron halves and set them aside to be filled and topped.

MARSHMALLOW FILLING

In the bowl of a stand mixer, combine the egg whites and sugar, and whisk together by hand until just combined. Set the bowl over the top of a simmering pot of water, making sure that a tight seal forms and that the bottom of the bowl is not actually touching the water.

Continuously whisk the mixture by hand while it heats up over the simmering water, heating it until it reaches 160°F (71°C) on a kitchen thermometer. When that temperature is reached, remove the bowl from the simmering water pot and place it onto your stand mixer. Beat the mixture on high, using the whisk attachment, for 4 to 5 minutes or until very stiff, glossy peaks are achieved. Add the vanilla, then beat for 10 more seconds to incorporate. Put the meringue in a piping bag fitted with a small star tip.

TOPPING AND ASSEMBLY

Dip the top of each perfect pair into the melted chocolate, then sprinkle with graham cracker crumbs. Allow the chocolate to fully set and harden.

Meanwhile, put the milk chocolate ganache in a piping bag fitted with a small round tip. Pipe a small amount of chocolate ganache into the center of each perfect pair bottom, then pipe around the chocolate ganache with the marshmallow filling.

When the chocolate on the tops has set, place each top onto its corresponding bottom. Carefully torch the marshmallow filling with a kitchen torch, then place the assembled macarons in the fridge to meld for 4 hours or overnight.

SOFT AND FLUFFY CARROT CAKE WHOOPIE PIES

There are two types of people in this world: those who like carrot cake and those who don't. I find that those who fall into the former group don't just like it, they love it. This whoopie pie recipe takes all the deliciousness of a carrot cake and transforms it into a small, handheld and portable little treat!

MAKES 12 TO 14 WHOOPIE PIES

CARROT CAKE WHOOPIE PIES

1 cup (110 g) finely shredded carrots

1 cup (220 g) packed brown sugar

¾ cup (180 ml) sour cream

½ cup (120 ml) vegetable oil

1 large egg

1 tsp vanilla extract

2 cups (250 g) all-purpose flour

½ tsp baking soda

¼ tsp table salt

1½ tsp (4 g) cinnamon

1 tsp allspice

½ tsp ground ginger

CREAM CHEESE FILLING

¼ cup (58 g) cream cheese, softened

2 tbsp (28 g) unsalted butter, at room temperature

1¼ cups (150 g) confectioners' sugar

½ tsp vanilla extract

CARROT CAKE WHOOPIE PIES

Preheat the oven to 350°F (175°C) and prepare two baking sheets with parchment. Place the shredded carrots into a clean kitchen towel and squeeze out as much excess water as you possibly can. Set the carrot aside.

In a large mixing bowl, combine the brown sugar, sour cream, vegetable oil, egg and vanilla. Whisk until very smooth.

In a separate bowl, combine the flour, baking soda, salt, cinnamon, allspice and ginger. Whisk until smooth.

Using a sieve, sift the dry ingredients into the bowl with the wet ingredients. Use a hand mixer to mix the dry ingredients into the wet. Mix only until everything is incorporated and smooth, but be careful not to overmix. Then add in the shredded carrot, and fold it into the batter.

Using a small, ¾-ounce (22-ml) cookie scoop, scoop little mounds of batter onto the prepared baking sheets (12 per sheet), ensuring there is about 2 inches (5 cm) of space between them.

Place baking sheets into the oven and bake for 11 minutes. When done, the cookies should have a springy top and a toothpick should come out clean. Allow to cool completely before filling.

CREAM CHEESE FILLING

In a medium mixing bowl, combine the cream cheese and butter. Beat together with a hand mixer until smooth. Add the confectioners' sugar and vanilla, then beat the filling until smooth. Transfer the filling to a piping bag.

Using your piping bag, cover half of the cookies with the filling, then place the others on top. Place into the fridge to meld together for 2 hours before enjoying.

VIBRANT RED VELVET WHOOPIE PIES

These red velvet–inspired whoopie pies will definitely make you say "whoopie!" Okay, but in all seriousness, this recipe is seriously outstanding. The definition of a truly fabulous dessert: two little mounds of bright red, moist cake sandwiched together with the king of all frostings—cream cheese frosting!

MAKES 12 TO 14 WHOOPIE PIES

RED VELVET WHOOPIE PIES

1 cup (220 g) packed brown sugar

¾ cup (180 ml) sour cream

½ cup (120 ml) vegetable oil

1 large egg

2 tbsp (30 ml) red food coloring

1 tsp vanilla extract

2 cups (250 g) all-purpose flour

3 tbsp (16 g) Dutch process cocoa powder, sifted

½ tsp baking soda

¼ tsp table salt

CREAM CHEESE FILLING

¼ cup (58 g) cream cheese, softened

2 tbsp (28 g) unsalted butter, at room temperature

1¼ cups (150 g) confectioners' sugar

½ tsp vanilla extract

RED VELVET WHOOPIE PIES

Preheat the oven to 350°F (175°C) and prepare two baking sheets with parchment. In a large mixing bowl, add the brown sugar, sour cream, vegetable oil, egg, red food coloring and vanilla. Whisk until very smooth.

In a separate bowl, combine the flour, sifted cocoa powder, baking soda and salt. Whisk until smooth.

Using a sieve, sift the dry ingredients into the bowl with the wet ingredients. Use a hand mixer to mix the dry ingredients into the wet. Mix only until everything is incorporated and smooth, and be careful not to overmix.

Using a small ¾-ounce (22-ml) cookie scoop, scoop little mounds of batter onto the prepared baking sheets (12 per sheet), ensuring there is about 2 inches (5 cm) of space between each.

Place the baking sheets into the oven and bake for 11 minutes. When done, the cookies should have a springy top, and a toothpick should come out clean. Allow to cool completely before filling.

CREAM CHEESE FILLING

In a medium mixing bowl, combine the cream cheese and butter. Beat together with a hand mixer until smooth looking. Add the confectioners' sugar and vanilla, then beat until smooth. Transfer the filling to a piping bag.

Using your piping bag, cover half of the cookies with the filling, then place the other cookies on top. Place into the fridge to meld together for 2 hours before enjoying.

FLUFFY BIRTHDAY CAKE MADELEINES

These delicious madeleines get their signature birthday cake flavor from the addition of tons of vanilla and a generous heaping of rainbow sprinkles. Don't skip that 15-minute freeze, as it's what gives madeleines their signature hump!

MAKES 20 COOKIES

BIRTHDAY CAKE MADELEINES

1 scant cup (115 g) all-purpose flour

½ tsp baking powder

¼ tsp table salt

2 large eggs

½ cup (100 g) white sugar

2 tsp (10 ml) vanilla extract

½ cup (120 ml) unsalted butter, melted

3 tbsp (36 g) sprinkles

VANILLA GLAZE

2 cups (240 g) confectioners' sugar

3 tbsp (45 ml) hot water

½ tsp vanilla extract

Sprinkles, for garnish

BIRTHDAY CAKE MADELEINES

Preheat the oven to 350°F (175°C). Prepare two madeleine pans by spraying them generously with baking spray, then brushing the baking spray over each cavity to ensure an even coating.

In a medium mixing bowl, combine the flour, baking powder and salt, then whisk together. Set aside.

In the bowl of a stand mixer fitted with the whisk attachment, combine the eggs, sugar and vanilla. Turn the stand mixer on high and whip the mixture for about 8 minutes. When done, the batter should look thick, be tripled in volume and ribbon off the attachment.

Remove the bowl from the stand mixer, then add the dry ingredients to it. Lightly fold the ingredients into the batter, only mixing until just combined and smooth. Pour the melted butter into a medium-sized bowl, then scoop some of the batter into the bowl and fold together. Pour that into the rest of the batter, and fold until combined again. Adding a small amount of batter into the melted butter helps lighten the butter, making it easier to combine with the remaining batter without deflating it. Finally, add the sprinkles and lightly fold them in.

Using a ¾-ounce (22-ml) cookie scoop, scoop the batter into the prepared madeleine pans, using the cookie scoop to lightly spread the batter into each madeleine cavity. Place the filled pans into the freezer for 15 minutes.

Remove the pans from the freezer and place into the oven to bake for 10 minutes. Remove the pans from the oven and allow the cookies to cool for 10 minutes in the pan, then carefully transfer the madeleines onto a cooling rack to finish cooling before glazing.

VANILLA GLAZE

Add the confectioners' sugar, hot water and vanilla to a medium mixing bowl. Whisk until the glaze comes together and is well combined. Dip half of each cooled madeleine into the glaze, then immediately garnish with sprinkles. Allow to set for about an hour before enjoying.

SPICED GINGERBREAD MADELEINES

Christmas cookies just got a major makeover with these gingerbread madeleines. They are full of those classic gingerbread flavors we all know and love—molasses, cinnamon and ginger—but come in a beautiful little spongey, buttery package. These spiced cookies are definitely best enjoyed on the day of baking!

MAKES 20 COOKIES

GINGERBREAD MADELEINES

1 scant cup (115 g) all-purpose flour

½ tsp baking powder

¼ tsp table salt

1½ tsp (4 g) cinnamon

¾ tsp ground ginger

¾ tsp allspice

2 large eggs

½ cup (100 g) white sugar

2 tsp (10 ml) fancy molasses

1 tsp vanilla extract

½ cup (120 ml) unsalted butter, melted

MOLASSES GLAZE

2 cups (240 g) confectioners' sugar

1 tsp fancy molasses

3 tbsp (45 ml) hot water

3 tbsp (21 g) crushed pecans, for garnish

GINGERBREAD MADELEINES

Preheat the oven to 350°F (175°C). Prepare two madeleine pans by spraying them generously with baking spray, then brushing the baking spray over each cavity to ensure an even coating.

In a medium mixing bowl, combine the flour, baking powder, salt, cinnamon, ground ginger and allspice, then whisk to combine. Set aside.

In the bowl of a stand mixer fitted with the whisk attachment, combine the eggs, sugar, molasses and vanilla. Turn the stand mixer on high and whip the mixture for about 8 minutes. When done, the batter should look thick, be tripled in volume and ribbon off the attachment.

Remove the bowl from the stand mixer, then add the dry ingredients to it. Lightly fold the dry ingredients into the batter, only mixing until just combined and smooth.

Pour the melted butter into a medium-sized bowl, then scoop some of the batter into the bowl and fold together. Then pour that into the rest of the batter, and fold until combined again.

Using a ¾-ounce (22-ml) cookie scoop, scoop the batter into the prepared madeleine pans, using the cookie scoop to lightly spread the batter into each madeleine cavity. Place the pans in the freezer for 15 minutes.

Remove the pans from the freezer and place in the oven to bake for 10 minutes. Remove from the oven and allow the madeleines to cool for 10 minutes in the pan, then carefully transfer the madeleines onto a cooling rack to finish cooling before glazing.

MOLASSES GLAZE

In a medium mixing bowl, combine the confectioners' sugar, molasses and hot water. Whisk until the glaze comes together and is well combined. Dip half of each cooled madeleine into the glaze, then immediately garnish with crushed pecans. Allow the glaze to set for about an hour before enjoying.

CAKE & CUPCAKE
Extravaganza

If you were to ask any of my family and friends what I am known for, they would unanimously say my cakes and cupcakes! I grew up with a huge affinity for creating different cake and cupcake flavors, so this chapter was definitely a special one for me. In this chapter, you will find cupcakes that are decorated with sky-high helpings of frosting, sheet cakes and loaves that are simplistic in nature but 100 percent guaranteed to delight from the first bite and, of course, layer cakes that can only be described as both beautiful and delicious!

CINNAMON LOVERS' CHURRO CUPCAKES

A churro, while surely delicious by itself, just isn't complete without a little dulce de leche for dipping on the side. These fluffy cupcakes reimagine classic churros with a cinnamon-infused cupcake that is topped with a truly incredible dulce de leche buttercream.

MAKES 12 CUPCAKES

CHURRO CUPCAKES

1⅓ cups (165 g) all-purpose flour

1¼ tsp (6 g) baking powder

½ tsp table salt

1½ tsp (4 g) cinnamon

½ cup (114 g) unsalted butter, at room temperature

1 cup (200 g) white sugar

1½ tsp (8 ml) vanilla extract

2 large eggs

½ cup (120 ml) buttermilk

CINNAMON-SUGAR TOPPING

1 tsp cinnamon

¼ cup (50 g) white sugar

2 tbsp (30 ml) unsalted butter, melted

DULCE DE LECHE BUTTERCREAM

1 cup (227 g) unsalted butter, at room temperature

½ tsp cinnamon

1⅓ cups (320 ml) dulce de leche, plus 2 tbsp (30 ml) for garnish

Note: If the buttercream looks liquid or loose, pop it into the fridge for 15 to 25 minutes, then beat again and it should come together!

CHURRO CUPCAKES

Preheat the oven to 350°F (175°C) and prepare a cupcake pan with liners (12 cupcakes total). In a large mixing bowl, combine the flour, baking powder, salt and cinnamon, then whisk together.

Into the bowl of a stand mixer fitted with the paddle attachment, place the butter, sugar and vanilla. Beat on medium-high until light and fluffy looking, 3 to 4 minutes. Add in the eggs, one at a time, beating well after each addition and scraping the sides of the bowl. Beat for an additional 2 minutes, or until the batter looks fluffy.

Add one-third of the flour mixture to the stand mixer and mix on low until combined. Add half of the buttermilk and mix on low until combined. Continue alternating the flour and the buttermilk, until both have been completely added, finishing with the flour mixture. Add the batter to the cupcake pans, filling each about two-thirds full, then bake in the oven for about 18 minutes or until a toothpick comes out clean. Allow the cupcakes to cool completely before topping and frosting.

CINNAMON-SUGAR TOPPING

In a small mixing bowl, whisk together the cinnamon and sugar until well combined. Brush the top of each cooled cupcake with melted butter, then sprinkle the cinnamon sugar over top.

DULCE DE LECHE BUTTERCREAM

In the bowl of a stand mixer fitted with the whisk attachment, combine the butter and cinnamon. Whip the butter on high for 5 minutes. When it's done, the butter should look fluffy and white.

Add the dulce de leche, in four additions, allowing the dulce de leche to completely incorporate before adding the next addition, 1 to 2 minutes between additions. When ready, the buttercream should look nice and fluffy. Transfer the buttercream to a piping bag with a tip, pipe the buttercream onto the cupcakes, then drizzle with additional dulce de leche.

LUSCIOUSLY SMOOTH CRÈME BRÛLÉE CUPCAKES

The quintessential flavors of crème brûlée? Creamy vanilla custard and the rich caramelly taste of the torched sugar topping. These crème brûlée cupcakes are stuffed with a creamy vanilla custard and topped with a burnt sugar buttercream, bringing together those classic crème brûlée flavors in cupcake form! It is best to make the vanilla custard first or even the day before—that way it has time to fully cool while you make everything else.

MAKES 20 CUPCAKES

VANILLA CUSTARD

2 large egg yolks

6 tbsp (90 g) white sugar

1 cup plus 2 tbsp (270 ml) half-and-half

2 tbsp (16 g) cornstarch

1 tbsp (14 g) unsalted butter, at room temperature

1 tsp vanilla bean paste or extract

Pinch table salt

CRÈME BRÛLÉE CUPCAKES

2¼ cups (280 g) all-purpose flour

1½ tsp (7 g) baking powder

½ tsp table salt

1½ cups (300 g) white sugar

3 large eggs

1 tsp vanilla extract

¾ cup (180 ml) vegetable oil

1 cup (240 ml) buttermilk

VANILLA CUSTARD

Put the egg yolks and white sugar in a medium saucepan. Whisk until smooth. Add in the half-and-half and cornstarch. Whisk again until smooth.

Place the saucepan on the stove over medium heat. Cook the mixture, whisking constantly, until it has thickened and just begins to bubble (it should resemble the thickness of pudding), then immediately remove it from the heat.

Whisk in the butter, vanilla and salt, then transfer the mixture to a heat-proof bowl. Place a piece of plastic wrap over the surface of the custard so a skin does not form, and place into the fridge to cool completely, for at least 4 hours.

CRÈME BRÛLÉE CUPCAKES

Preheat the oven to 350°F (175°C) and prepare two cupcake pans with liners (20 cupcakes total). In a large mixing bowl, add the flour, baking powder and salt, then whisk together to combine.

In the bowl of a stand mixer fitted with the paddle attachment, combine the sugar, eggs and vanilla. Beat on high for about 5 minutes—the mixture should look thick, fluffy and tripled in volume. Then, slowly drizzle in the oil. After all the oil has been added, beat for an additional minute.

While running the mixer on low, add the dry mixture in three additions, alternating with the buttermilk in between. Beat only until the batter becomes smooth. Add the batter to the cupcake pans (filling each about two-thirds full), then bake the cupcakes in the oven for about 18 minutes or until a toothpick comes out clean. Allow them to cool completely before filling and frosting.

Once cooled, using a cupcake corer, paring knife or the backside of a piping tip, cut out a 1- to 2-inch (2.5- to 5-cm) deep piece from the top of each cupcake, and fill each hole with 1 tablespoon (15 ml) of custard.

(continued)

LUSCIOUSLY SMOOTH CRÈME BRÛLÉE CUPCAKES (CONTINUED)

BURNT SUGAR BUTTERCREAM

1½ cups (300 g) white sugar

½ cup (120 ml) boiling water

1½ cups (340 g) unsalted butter, at room temperature

3¾ cups (450 g) confectioners' sugar

1½ tsp (8 ml) vanilla extract

BURNT SUGAR BUTTERCREAM

Put the white sugar in a tall, wide-bottomed pot over medium heat. Stir the sugar with a wooden spoon constantly while it heats up, breaking up any clumps as they form. The sugar will eventually melt down into an amber-colored syrup.

When an amber color has been achieved, remove the pot from the heat and very slowly and very carefully drizzle in the boiling water, stirring vigorously as you drizzle (be careful, as it will bubble and steam a lot). Once all of the water has been added and the syrup is smooth, pour the syrup into a heatproof container and allow it to cool to at least room temperature in the fridge, about 4 hours.

When the syrup is at room temperature, add the butter to a stand mixer fitted with the whisk attachment or a large bowl. Beat on high until the butter is doubled in volume and looks light and fluffy, 3 to 5 minutes.

Turn the stand mixer to low and slowly add the confectioners' sugar and vanilla. Turn the mixer up to medium, then beat until completely incorporated and smooth.

Add in the burnt sugar syrup in two additions, fully incorporating the first before adding the second. Beat until everything is well combined and fully incorporated, then transfer to a piping bag and pipe onto the filled cupcakes.

DREAMY COCONUT CREAM LAYER CAKE

Three thick layers of moist, tender coconut cake, sandwiched together with a silky coconut pastry cream, then smothered in coconut buttercream and perfectly toasted pieces of sweet shredded coconut. Sounds like a dream, now, doesn't it? I suggest making the coconut pastry cream first or even the day before. That way it has time to fully cool while you make everything else!

MAKES 1 (8-INCH [20-CM]) CAKE

COCONUT PASTRY CREAM

5 large egg yolks

¾ cup (150 g) white sugar

2 cups (480 ml) full-fat coconut milk, well mixed and smooth

¼ cup (32 g) cornstarch

½ cup (47 g) sweetened shredded coconut

1 tbsp (14 g) unsalted butter, at room temperature

1½ tsp (7.5 ml) vanilla extract

¾ tsp coconut extract

¼ tsp table salt

COCONUT CAKE

4½ cups (560 g) all-purpose flour

1 tbsp (14 g) baking powder

1 tsp table salt

3 cups (600 g) white sugar

6 large eggs

4 tsp (20 ml) coconut extract

1 tsp vanilla extract

1¾ cups (420 ml) vegetable oil

2 cups (480 ml) full-fat coconut milk, well mixed to be smooth

1 cup (93 g) sweetened shredded coconut

COCONUT PASTRY CREAM

In a medium saucepan, combine the egg yolks and white sugar. Whisk until smooth. Add in the coconut milk and cornstarch. Whisk again until smooth. Place the saucepan on the stove over medium heat. Cook the mixture, whisking constantly, until it has thickened and just begins to bubble (it should resemble the thickness of pudding). Once the pastry cream is bubbling, continue to cook for exactly 1 minute, then remove from the heat immediately.

Whisk in the shredded coconut, butter, vanilla, coconut extract and salt, then place the pastry cream into a heatproof bowl. Place a piece of plastic wrap over the surface of the pastry cream so a skin does not form, and place into the fridge to cool completely, at least 4 to 6 hours or preferably overnight.

COCONUT CAKE

Preheat the oven to 350°F (175°C), and prepare three 8-inch (20-cm) springform cake pans with cooking spray and parchment on the bottom. In a large mixing bowl, add the flour, baking powder and salt, then whisk together to combine.

In the bowl of a stand mixer fitted with the paddle attachment, combine the sugar, eggs, coconut extract and vanilla. Beat on high for about 5 minutes—the mixture should look thick, fluffy and tripled in volume. Then, slowly drizzle in the oil. After all the oil has been added, beat for an additional minute.

Running the mixer on low, add the dry mixture in three additions, alternating with the coconut milk in between. Beat only until the batter becomes smooth. Fold in the sweetened shredded coconut, then add the batter in equal amounts into the pans. Bake in the oven for 35 to 40 minutes, or until an inserted toothpick comes out clean. Allow the cake to cool completely before filling and frosting.

(continued)

COCONUT BUTTERCREAM

1¾ cups (397 g) unsalted butter, at room temperature

7 cups (840 g) confectioners' sugar

6 tbsp (90 ml) full-fat coconut milk, well mixed and smooth

1¾ tsp (9 ml) vanilla extract

1¾ tsp (9 ml) coconut extract

1½ cups (140 g) sweetened shredded coconut

COCONUT BUTTERCREAM

Put the butter in the bowl of a stand mixer fitted with the whisk attachment. Beat on high for 2 minutes.

Turn the stand mixer to low and slowly add the confectioners' sugar. Beat until completely incorporated, then add in the coconut milk, vanilla and coconut extract. Beat until well combined and fully incorporated.

TOASTED COCONUT TOPPING

Meanwhile, place a dry pan on the stove over medium-high heat and heat until very hot. Working in four to five batches, add the sweetened shredded coconut. Toss and stir the coconut until it is well toasted and golden brown. Transfer the batches of toasted coconut onto a plate to cool to room temperature and continue onto the next batch until all of the coconut has been toasted.

ASSEMBLY

Level off each of the cake layers to remove any doming from the cakes.

Place one cake layer onto your serving plate. Add a quarter of the buttercream to a piping bag, then pipe a buttercream dam atop the perimeter of the cake layer. Add ½ cup (120 ml) of the coconut pastry cream into the center of the dam and spread it out evenly.

Add the second layer on top, then repeat the previous step.

Add the final layer onto the cake, then frost the outside and top with the remaining buttercream. Pat the toasted coconut shreds onto the outside of the cake. Place the cake into the fridge for at least 3 hours to set up. Keep the cake in the fridge for storing.

BROWN BUTTER BANANA BREAD SHEET CAKE

There's nothing quite like a dessert that is easy to make, incredibly delicious and simple
to decorate and transport! Sheet cakes tick every one of those boxes. The best part?
The creamy, intensely chocolatey ganache frosting on top!

MAKES 1 (9 X 13-INCH [20 X 23-CM]) SHEET CAKE

CHOCOLATE GANACHE FROSTING

1 cup (240 ml) heavy cream

¾ cup (150 g) white sugar

6 tbsp (85 g) unsalted butter, at room temperature

6 oz (170 g) semisweet chocolate, finely chopped

¾ tsp vanilla extract

BANANA BREAD SHEET CAKE

½ cup (114 g) unsalted butter, at room temperature

2 cups (250 g) all-purpose flour

2 tsp (9 g) baking powder

1 tsp baking soda

½ tsp table salt

½ tsp cinnamon

1¼ cups (275 g) packed dark brown sugar

1 cup plus 2 tbsp (260 ml) mashed overripe bananas

¾ cup (180 ml) sour cream

½ cup (120 ml) vegetable oil

3 large eggs

1½ tsp (8 ml) vanilla extract

1 banana, sliced, for decorating

⅓ cup (39 g) walnuts or pecans, for decorating

CHOCOLATE GANACHE FROSTING

In a medium saucepan over medium heat, combine the cream, sugar and butter. Heat until the mixture begins to bubble.

Put the chopped chocolate in a medium heatproof mixing bowl, then pour the hot liquid over it. Stir lightly with a spatula, then let the mixture sit for 3 minutes to melt the chocolate. After 3 minutes, add the vanilla and then whisk the ganache until smooth. Cover the ganache with plastic wrap, then place it into the fridge to cool for at least 3 to 4 hours, or preferably overnight.

BANANA BREAD SHEET CAKE

In a small saucepan over medium heat, bring the butter to a boil. Continue heating, stirring constantly, until the butter has turned a nutty brown color. It may be hard to see the color if your butter is foaming a lot, so periodically take it off the heat to check the color. Remove the butter from the heat and place it in a heatproof bowl to cool for 15 minutes.

Preheat the oven to 350°F (175°C). Prepare a 9 x 13–inch (23 x 33–cm) baking sheet with cooking spray and parchment. In a medium bowl, combine the flour, baking powder, baking soda, salt and cinnamon. Whisk until well combined. Set aside.

In a separate large mixing bowl, combine the browned butter, brown sugar, mashed bananas, sour cream, vegetable oil, eggs and vanilla, then whisk until well combined. Add the dry ingredients to the wet ingredients, then whisk until a smooth batter comes together. Pour the batter into the prepared baking sheet and bake for about 30 minutes, or until an inserted toothpick comes out clean. Allow the cake to cool completely before frosting.

Remove the ganache from the fridge and transfer it to a stand mixer. Beat on high with the whisk attachment until fluffy. Smooth the ganache over the cooled cake with a spatula and garnish with the sliced banana and nuts.

DEVILISHLY GOOD BOSTON CREAM CUPCAKES

Boston Cream Pie is a classic American dessert that features two moist cake layers
sandwiched together with custard or pastry cream and then topped with chocolate ganache.
Yum, right? It just seemed like a no-brainer to make this classic dessert in cupcake form!
This recipe features a delectably moist vanilla cupcake that is stuffed full of a rich, velvety
pastry cream and topped with a whipped chocolate ganache frosting! It is best to make the
vanilla pastry cream and chocolate ganache frosting first or even the day before. That way,
they have time to fully cool while you make the cupcakes.

MAKES 20 CUPCAKES

VANILLA PASTRY CREAM

2 large egg yolks

3 tbsp (15 g) white sugar

1 cup plus 2 tbsp (270 ml)
half-and-half

2 tbsp (16 g) cornstarch

1 tbsp (14 g) unsalted butter, at
room temperature

¾ tsp vanilla extract

Pinch table salt

CHOCOLATE GANACHE
FROSTING

1½ cups (360 ml) heavy cream

1 cup (200 g) white sugar

9 tbsp (128 g) unsalted butter, at
room temperature

9 oz (255 g) semisweet chocolate,
finely chopped

1 tsp vanilla extract

VANILLA PASTRY CREAM

In a medium saucepan, combine the egg yolks and white sugar. Whisk
until smooth. Add in the half-and-half and cornstarch. Whisk again until
smooth.

Place the saucepan on the stove over medium heat. Cook the mixture,
whisking constantly, until it has thickened and just begins to bubble (it
should resemble the thickness of pudding). Once the pastry cream is
bubbling, continue to cook for exactly 1 minute, then remove from the
heat immediately.

Add in the butter, vanilla and salt, then transfer to a heatproof bowl.
Place a piece of plastic wrap over the surface of the pastry cream so
a skin does not form, then place into the fridge to cool completely, at
least 4 hours or preferably overnight.

CHOCOLATE GANACHE FROSTING

In a medium saucepan over medium heat, combine the cream, sugar
and butter. Heat until the mixture begins to bubble.

Put the chopped chocolate in a medium heatproof mixing bowl, then pour
the hot liquid over the top. Stir lightly with a spatula, then let the mixture
sit for 3 minutes to melt the chocolate. After 3 minutes, add the vanilla and
then whisk the ganache together until incorporated and smooth.

Cover the ganache with plastic wrap, then place into the fridge to cool
for at least 3 to 4 hours, or overnight.

(continued)

DEVILISHLY GOOD BOSTON CREAM CUPCAKES (CONTINUED)

BOSTON CREAM CUPCAKES

2¼ cups (280 g) all-purpose flour
1½ tsp (7 g) baking powder
½ tsp table salt
1½ cups (300 g) white sugar
3 large eggs
1 tsp vanilla extract
¾ cup (180 ml) vegetable oil
1 cup (240 ml) buttermilk

Sprinkles (optional)

BOSTON CREAM CUPCAKES

Preheat the oven to 350°F (175°C), and prepare two cupcake pans with liners (20 cupcakes total). In a large mixing bowl, whisk together the flour, baking powder and salt.

In the bowl of a stand mixer fitted with the paddle attachment, beat the sugar, eggs and vanilla on high for about 5 minutes—the mixture should look thick, fluffy and tripled in volume. Then slowly drizzle in the oil. After all the oil has been added, beat for an additional minute.

While running the stand mixer on low, add the dry mixture in three additions, alternating with the buttermilk in between. Beat only until the batter becomes smooth. Add the batter to the cupcake pans (filling each about two-thirds full), then bake in the oven for about 18 minutes, or until a toothpick comes out clean. Allow the cupcakes to cool completely before filling and frosting.

FROSTING AND ASSEMBLY

Once the cupcakes and pastry cream have fully cooled, use a cupcake corer, paring knife or the backside of a piping tip to cut out an approximately 1- to 2-inch (2.5- to 5-cm) deep piece from the top of each cupcake. Fill each hole with 1 tablespoon (15 ml) of pastry cream.

Remove the cold ganache from the fridge and transfer to a stand mixer with the whisk attachment. Beat on high until fluffy looking. Transfer to a piping bag, pipe the ganache onto the filled cupcakes, then garnish with sprinkles, if desired.

Enjoy the cupcakes that day, or keep in the fridge if storing.

TOASTY S'MORES CUPCAKES

This chocolate cupcake sits atop a buttery graham cracker base, topped with a silky chocolate buttercream and ganache, and filled with a light and airy marshmallow filling. The addition of fresh hot coffee in the batter helps to intensify the chocolate flavor, giving these cupcakes even more of a fudgy oomph! If these s'mores cupcakes had a middle name, it would be "decadent!"

MAKES 18 CUPCAKES

GRAHAM CRACKER BASE

1½ cups (200 g) graham cracker crumbs

2 tbsp (30 g) white sugar

6 tbsp (90 ml) unsalted butter, melted

CHOCOLATE CUPCAKES

1¼ cups (150 g) all-purpose flour

½ tsp baking soda

½ tsp baking powder

¼ tsp table salt

1 large egg

1 cup (200 g) white sugar

½ cup (120 ml) sour cream

¼ cup (60 ml) vegetable oil

1 tsp vanilla extract

6 tbsp (90 ml) hot freshly brewed coffee

6 tbsp (32 g) Dutch process cocoa powder (regular cocoa can be used, too)

GRAHAM CRACKER BASE

Preheat the oven to 350°F (175°C), and prepare two cupcake pans with liners (18 cupcakes total). Combine the graham cracker crumbs and sugar in a bowl and whisk until well combined. Pour in the melted butter, then mix with a fork, or your hands, until the butter is well dispersed and the mixture resembles wet sand. Spoon 2 tablespoons (30 ml) of graham cracker crust into each cupcake liner, then press down with a ¼-cup (60-ml) measuring cup to flatten. Place into the oven to bake for 8 minutes. Allow to cool while you make the cupcake batter.

CHOCOLATE CUPCAKES

In a large mixing bowl, combine the flour, baking soda, baking powder and salt. Whisk together to combine. Set aside.

In another large bowl, combine the egg, sugar, sour cream, vegetable oil and vanilla. Whisk together until smooth and well combined.

In a small mixing bowl or 2-cup (480-ml) liquid measuring cup, combine the hot coffee and cocoa powder. Whisk together until well combined and smooth. Allow it to sit for 2 minutes, then add the cocoa mixture into the mixing bowl with the wet ingredients and mix until smooth.

Add the wet ingredients to the bowl with the dry ingredients, and mix until smooth. Pour the batter over the tops of the graham cracker crusts in the cupcake pan, stopping when each one is two-thirds full. Then bake for 16 to 18 minutes, or until an inserted toothpick comes out clean. Allow the cupcakes to cool completely before filling and frosting.

(continued)

CHOCOLATE BUTTERCREAM

1⅓ cups (302 g) unsalted butter, at room temperature

4½ cups (540 g) confectioners' sugar

⅔ cup (50 g) Dutch process cocoa powder, sifted

Pinch table salt

¼ cup (60 ml) heavy cream

¾ tsp vanilla extract

MILK CHOCOLATE TOPPING

¾ cup (126 g) milk chocolate chips

1 tbsp (14 g) coconut oil

MARSHMALLOW FILLING AND TOPPING

⅔ cup (160 g) fresh egg whites

1¼ cups (250 g) white sugar

CHOCOLATE BUTTERCREAM

Put the butter in the bowl of a stand mixer fitted with the whisk attachment or a large bowl. Beat on high until the butter is doubled in volume and looks light and fluffy, 3 to 5 minutes.

Turn the stand mixer or hand mixer to low and slowly add the confectioners' sugar, cocoa powder and salt. Beat on medium until completely incorporated and smooth.

Add in the heavy cream and vanilla. Beat until well combined and fully incorporated, then add to a piping bag to pipe onto the cupcakes after they have been filled.

MILK CHOCOLATE TOPPING

Add the chocolate chips and coconut oil to a microwave-proof bowl and place in the microwave for 1 to 2 minutes, or until melted (check at 1 minute, stir and return to the microwave if needed). Set aside while you make the marshmallow filling and topping.

MARSHMALLOW FILLING AND TOPPING

Put the egg whites and sugar in the bowl of your stand mixer and whisk together. Set the bowl over the top of a simmering pot of water, making sure to form a tight seal and that the bottom of the stand mixer bowl is not actually touching the water.

Continuously whisk the mixture by hand while it heats up over the simmering water, heating it until it reaches 160°F (71°C) on a kitchen thermometer. When that temperature is reached, remove the bowl from the simmering water pot and place onto your stand mixer. Using the whisk attachment, beat the mixture on high for 4 to 5 minutes or until stiff, glossy peaks are achieved. Place the filling into a piping bag fitted with a closed star tip.

ASSEMBLY

Using a cupcake corer, paring knife or the backside of a piping tip, cut out an approximately 1- to 2-inch (2.5- to 5-cm) deep piece from the top of each cupcake, and fill each with 1 to 2 tablespoons (15 to 30 ml) of marshmallow filling.

Pipe the chocolate buttercream onto each filled cupcake, then top the buttercream with a spoonful of milk chocolate topping. Finally, using the rest of the marshmallow filling, pipe a marshmallow hat onto the top of each cupcake. Using a kitchen torch, toast the marshmallow hat.

EPIC LEMON MERINGUE CAKE

Lemon lovers, rejoice! This lemon meringue cake was made for you: Three thick layers of
fluffy cake, with that mouthwatering tangy lemon flavor, are stacked together and filled
with a creamy, tart lemon curd. And it wouldn't be lemon meringue without the meringue!
Instead of a typical buttercream, this cake is frosted with meringue, which is then torched
to golden perfection. If you prefer a lemon curd that is less lemony, replace 1 tablespoon
(15 ml) of the lemon juice with water. I suggest making the lemon curd first or even the
day before. That way it has time to fully cool while you make everything else.

MAKES 1 (6-INCH [15-CM]) CAKE

LEMON CURD

1 large egg

1 large egg yolk

½ cup (100 g) white sugar

¼ cup (60 ml) fresh lemon juice

2 tbsp (30 ml) unsalted butter, melted

LEMON CAKE

3 cups (375 g) all-purpose flour

2 tsp (9 g) baking powder

½ tsp table salt

Juice of ½ lemon

1⅓ cups (320 ml) buttermilk

2 cups (400 g) white sugar

4 large eggs

1½ tsp (7.5 ml) vanilla extract

1 cup (240 ml) vegetable oil

LEMON CURD

In a medium saucepan, combine the egg, egg yolk, white sugar, lemon
juice and melted butter. Whisk until smooth.

Place the saucepan on the stove over medium heat. Cook the mixture,
whisking constantly, until the mixture begins to bubble. Once the curd
begins to bubble, continue cooking for exactly 1 minute, then immediately remove from the heat. The curd should look thickened.

Transfer the curd to a bowl and place a piece of plastic wrap over the
surface of the curd so a skin does not form. Put the bowl into the fridge
to cool completely, at least 4 hours, but preferably overnight.

LEMON CAKE

Preheat the oven to 350°F (175°C), and prepare three 6-inch (15-cm)
springform cake pans with cooking spray and parchment rounds. In a
large mixing bowl, whisk together the flour, baking powder and salt.
Set aside.

Add the lemon juice to the buttermilk and set aside.

In the bowl of a stand mixer fitted with the paddle attachment, put the
sugar, eggs and vanilla. Beat on high for about 5 minutes—the mixture
should look thick, fluffy and tripled in volume. Then, slowly drizzle in the
oil. After all the oil has been added, beat for an additional minute.

While running the stand mixer on low, add the dry mixture in three
additions, alternating with the buttermilk mixture in between. Beat
only until the batter becomes smooth. Pour the batter evenly into the
cake pans and then bake in the oven for 30 to 35 minutes, or until a
toothpick inserted in the center comes out clean. Allow the cakes to
cool completely before filling, frosting and stacking.

(continued)

MERINGUE

⅔ cup (160 g) fresh egg whites

1¼ cups (225 g) white sugar

MERINGUE

Put the egg whites and sugar in the bowl of your stand mixer and whisk them together. Set the bowl over the top of a simmering pot of water, making sure to form a tight seal and that the bottom of the stand mixer bowl is not actually touching the water.

Continuously whisk the mixture by hand while it heats up over the simmering water, heating it until it reaches 160°F (71°C) on a kitchen thermometer. When the temperature is reached, remove the bowl from the simmering water pot and place it onto your stand mixer. Using the whisk attachment, beat the mixture on high for 4 to 5 minutes or until very stiff, glossy peaks are achieved.

ASSEMBLY

Level off each of the cake layers to remove any doming from the cakes.

Place one cake layer onto your serving plate. Add a quarter of the meringue to a piping bag, then pipe a meringue dam atop the perimeter of the cake layer. Add half of the lemon curd into the center of the dam and spread it out evenly.

Add the second layer on top, then repeat the previous step.

Add the final layer onto the cake, then frost the outside and top with the remaining meringue. Use a kitchen torch to toast the meringue. Enjoy immediately or store in the fridge.

Note: *It is best to use a hot knife to slice this cake, otherwise the meringue likes to stick to the knife.*

RICH AND CREAMY TIRAMISU CHOCOLATE CUPCAKES

Coffee connoisseurs, say hello to your new favorite treat! These insanely decadent chocolate cupcakes are filled with a sweet and creamy mascarpone custard filling, and topped with a coffee and Kahlúa–spiked buttercream, bringing together all those delicious, classic tiramisu flavors! I suggest making the mascarpone custard first or even the day before. That way it has time to fully cool while you make everything else.

MAKES 12 CUPCAKES

MASCARPONE CUSTARD FILLING

3 large egg yolks

6 tbsp (75 g) white sugar

⅓ cup (80 ml) whole milk

1 cup (232 g) mascarpone cheese, softened

1 tsp vanilla extract

CHOCOLATE CUPCAKES

1¼ cups (150 g) all-purpose flour

1 tsp instant coffee powder

½ tsp baking soda

½ tsp baking powder

¼ tsp table salt

1 large egg

1 cup (200 g) white sugar

½ cup (120 ml) sour cream

¼ cup (60 ml) vegetable oil

1 tsp vanilla extract

6 tbsp (90 ml) hot freshly brewed coffee

6 tbsp (32 g) Dutch process cocoa powder, plus extra for garnish (regular cocoa can be used, too)

MASCARPONE CUSTARD FILLING

In a medium saucepan, whisk together the egg yolks, white sugar and milk.

Place the saucepan on the stove over medium heat. Cook the mixture, whisking constantly, until it has thickened and just begins to bubble, then cook for exactly 15 seconds longer. Remove from the heat immediately after.

Transfer the custard to a bowl and place a piece of plastic wrap over the surface of the custard so a skin does not form. Place into the fridge to cool completely, at least 4 to 6 hours, or preferably overnight.

When the custard is sufficiently cooled, put the mascarpone cheese and vanilla into a large mixing bowl. Beat until smooth and creamy looking. Pour this into the cooled custard, then beat until well combined and smooth.

CHOCOLATE CUPCAKES

Preheat the oven to 350°F (175°C), and prepare a cupcake pan with liners (12 cupcakes total). In a large mixing bowl, whisk together the flour, coffee powder, baking soda, baking powder and salt. Set aside.

In another large bowl, add the egg, sugar, sour cream, vegetable oil and vanilla. Whisk together until smooth and well combined.

In a small mixing bowl or 2-cup (480-ml) liquid measuring cup, put the hot coffee and cocoa powder. Whisk together until well combined and smooth. Allow to sit for 2 minutes, then add the cocoa mixture to the mixing bowl with the wet ingredients and mix until smooth.

(continued)

COFFEE BUTTERCREAM

1 cup (227 g) unsalted butter, at room temperature

3½ cups (420 g) confectioners' sugar

¼ cup (60 ml) Kahlúa (can substitute with cold strong coffee)

1½ tsp (3 g) instant coffee powder

½ tsp vanilla extract

Pinch table salt

Add the wet ingredients into the bowl with the dry ingredients, and mix until smooth. Pour the batter into the prepared cupcake pan, stopping when each cupcake cavity is two-thirds full, then bake for 18 to 20 minutes or until an inserted toothpick comes out clean. Allow the cupcakes to cool completely before filling and frosting.

COFFEE BUTTERCREAM

Put the butter into a stand mixer fitted with the whisk attachment. Beat on high until the butter is doubled in volume and looks light and fluffy, about 5 minutes.

Turn the stand mixer to low and slowly add the confectioners' sugar. Beat until completely incorporated, then add in the Kahlúa, coffee powder, vanilla and salt. Beat until well combined and fully incorporated.

Place the coffee buttercream into a piping bag fitted with a star tip.

ASSEMBLY

Using a cupcake corer, paring knife or the backside of a piping tip, cut out an approximately 1- to 2-inch (2.5- to 5-cm) deep piece from the top of each cupcake, and fill each hole with 1 to 2 tablespoons (15 to 30 ml) of mascarpone custard. Finally, pipe the coffee buttercream onto each filled cupcake and dust them with some additional cocoa powder.

DECADENT BANANAS FOSTER LAYER CAKE

Bananas Foster is a dessert with origins in New Orleans, circa 1951. The classic dessert is made from bananas that are cooked in a buttery caramel sauce, then flambéed with a little dark rum and served with vanilla ice cream. This recipe transforms all that into layer cake form! Rich, moist banana cake is smooshed together with a classic bananas Foster filling, frosted and then topped with a deeply sweet salted caramel sauce.

MAKES 1 (6-INCH [15-CM]) CAKE

SALTED CARAMEL

½ cup (100 g) white sugar

2 tbsp (30 ml) water

3 tbsp (43 g) unsalted butter, at room temperature and cubed

¼ cup (60 ml) heavy cream

½ tsp vanilla extract

½ tsp table salt

SALTED CARAMEL

Put the sugar and water into a large saucepan over medium heat. Stir occasionally until the sugar has dissolved and the mixture begins to boil.

Once the mixture begins to boil, turn the heat up to medium-high and allow the mixture to boil, being careful not to stir it, until it turns amber in color (stirring the mixture will cause crystallization, so refrain from stirring).

Once the mixture has become amber in color (360°F [182°C] on a candy thermometer), add the cubed butter and mix very vigorously to combine. (Be careful, however, because the mixture will bubble and rise up rapidly when you add the butter.) If the butter seems to be separating from the caramel, remove it from the heat and whisk vigorously until it comes together.

Next, slowly drizzle in the heavy cream (it will bubble rapidly again) while whisking. Then add the vanilla and salt. Whisk until smooth and well combined. Remove the caramel from the heat, then set aside to cool to room temperature, about 4 hours.

(continued)

BANANAS FOSTER FILLING

⅔ cup (145 g) packed dark brown sugar

¼ cup (57 g) unsalted butter, at room temperature

3 tbsp (45 ml) water

¼ tsp cinnamon

2 slightly underripe bananas, sliced into ½-inch (1.3-cm) slices, plus more for garnish

6 tbsp (90 ml) dark rum

1 tsp vanilla extract

½ tsp banana extract

BANANA CAKE

2⅓ cups (320 g) all-purpose flour

2 tsp (9 g) baking powder

1½ tsp (7 g) baking soda

¾ tsp table salt

1⅓ cups (320 ml) vegetable oil

1¼ cups (275 g) packed dark brown sugar

1½ cups (320 ml) puréed overripe bananas

1 cup (240 ml) sour cream

4 large eggs

2 tsp (10 ml) vanilla extract

BANANAS FOSTER FILLING

In a large pan over medium heat, combine the brown sugar, butter, water and cinnamon. Heat the mixture, while continuously stirring, until the brown sugar fully dissolves and is no longer grainy, 5 to 7 minutes.

Add the sliced bananas to the pan and toss to coat them in the sugar syrup. Continue cooking, while gently moving the bananas around, until the bananas soften and begin to brown.

Remove the pan from the heat source, then add the rum. Using a long-stemmed lighter, carefully ignite the rum. Carefully return the pan back to the heat, and gently shake the pan until the flames dissipate.

Continue heating while stirring or shaking, for an additional 3 minutes, then remove from the heat and add in the vanilla and banana extract.

Transfer the bananas Foster into a bowl and let it come to room temperature—3 to 4 hours.

BANANA CAKE

Preheat the oven to 350°F (175°C). Prepare three 6-inch (15-cm) spring-form cake pans with cooking spray and parchment. In a medium bowl, whisk together the flour, baking powder, baking soda and salt. Set aside.

In a separate large mixing bowl, add the vegetable oil, brown sugar, puréed bananas, sour cream, eggs and vanilla. Whisk until well combined and smooth.

Add the dry ingredients to the large bowl with the wet ingredients, then whisk until a smooth batter comes together.

Divide the batter evenly between the three prepared pans, then place them in the oven to bake for about 35 minutes, or until an inserted toothpick comes out clean. Allow the cakes to cool completely before filling and frosting.

½ cup (120 g) fresh egg whites

1⅔ cups (266 g) white sugar

1½ cups (340 g) unsalted butter, at room temperature

2 tsp (10 ml) vanilla extract

Pinch table salt

SWISS MERINGUE BUTTERCREAM

Put the egg whites and sugar in the bowl of your stand mixer and whisk together. Set the bowl over the top of a simmering pot of water, making sure to form a tight seal and that the bottom of the stand mixer bowl is not actually touching the water.

Continuously whisk the mixture by hand while it heats up over the simmering water, heating it until it reaches 160°F (71°C) on a kitchen thermometer. When the temperature is reached, remove the bowl from the simmering water pot and place it onto your stand mixer. Using the whisk attachment, beat the mixture on high for 4 to 5 minutes or until very stiff, glossy peaks form.

Turn the stand mixer to low and add in the butter 2 tablespoons (28 g) at a time, allowing each addition to incorporate a bit before the next. When all of the butter has been added, turn the stand mixer back onto high and beat until the buttercream looks smooth. (It may look curdled and soupy at one point, but just keep beating.)

Finally, add in the vanilla and salt, then quickly beat to incorporate.

ASSEMBLY

Level off each of the cake layers to remove any doming from the cakes. Spread a thin layer of buttercream onto the cut surface of each cake.

Place one cake layer onto your serving plate, buttercream side up. Add a quarter of the buttercream to a piping bag, then pipe a buttercream dam atop the perimeter of the cake layer. Add one-third of the bananas Foster filling into the center of the dam and spread it out evenly.

Add the second layer on top, then repeat the previous step.

Add the final layer onto the cake, buttercream side down, then evenly frost the outside and top with the remaining buttercream. Pour the salted caramel over the top of the cake and let it drip down the sides, then add more sliced bananas on top.

ULTRA-MOIST PUMPKIN LOAF CAKE

I know that pumpkin pie gets all the fame, but pumpkin is such a versatile ingredient and its flavor can be adapted into so many different treats! This pumpkin loaf takes all the goodness you know and love about pumpkin pie, and turns it into a moist, tender and perfectly spiced loaf cake. This pumpkin loaf is great by itself, but after you've enjoyed it with a little sweetened whipped cream, you'll soon be saying, "Pumpkin pie who?"

MAKES 1 (9 X 5-INCH [23 X 13-CM]) LOAF

2 cups (240 g) all-purpose flour

1 cup (220 g) packed dark brown sugar

½ cup (100 g) white sugar

2 tsp (9 g) baking powder

1 tsp baking soda

½ tsp table salt

2 tsp (5 g) cinnamon

1 tsp allspice

½ tsp ground ginger

¼ tsp nutmeg

3 large eggs, at room temperature

1 (15-oz [450-ml]) can pumpkin purée

1 cup (240 ml) unsalted butter, melted

1 tsp vanilla extract

Whipped cream (optional)

Preheat the oven to 350°F (175°C). Prepare a 9 x 5–inch (23 x 13–cm) loaf pan with cooking spray and parchment. In a medium bowl, combine the flour, brown sugar, white sugar, baking powder, baking soda, salt, cinnamon, allspice, ginger and nutmeg and whisk together. Set aside.

In a separate large mixing bowl, put the eggs, pumpkin purée, melted butter and vanilla. Whisk until well combined and smooth.

Add the dry ingredients to the large bowl with the wet ingredients, then whisk until a smooth batter comes together.

Pour the batter into the prepared pan, then place into the oven to bake for 60 to 65 minutes, or until an inserted toothpick comes out clean. Allow the cake to cool completely before slicing. Enjoy with some lightly sweetened whipped cream or whipped topping.

CINNAMON-SWIRLED BUTTER PECAN BUNDT CAKE

I am a huge sucker for elegant layer cakes. But sometimes I crave a cake that is equally as beautiful, but without all the fussy stacking, leveling and frosting. Enter Bundt cakes! This truly breath-taking butter pecan swirl Bundt cake is made with a tender, buttery cake speckled with tiny pieces of pecan and topped with a dulce de leche glaze that stays soft and creamy.

MAKES 1 (10-INCH [25-CM]) BUNDT CAKE

PECAN SWIRL
⅔ cup (145 g) packed dark brown sugar
⅓ cup (36 g) finely chopped pecans
1 tsp cinnamon

BUTTER PECAN BUNDT
2⅓ cups (320 g) all-purpose flour
2 tsp (9 g) baking powder
1 tsp baking soda
1 tsp table salt
1½ cups (340 g) unsalted butter, at room temperature
1½ cups (300 g) white sugar
2 tbsp (30 ml) maple syrup
2 tsp (10 ml) vanilla extract
½ tsp maple extract
4 large eggs
1 cup (240 ml) sour cream
1 cup (109 g) pecans, chopped

GLAZE
1 cup (120 g) confectioners' sugar
⅔ cup (160 ml) dulce de leche
1 to 2 tbsp (15 to 30 ml) heavy cream, depending on desired consistency

PECAN SWIRL

In a small mixing bowl, combine all of the pecan swirl ingredients and whisk together. Set aside for later.

BUTTER PECAN BUNDT

Preheat the oven to 350°F (175°C), and prepare a 10-inch (25-cm) Bundt pan with baking spray. In a large mixing bowl, combine the flour, baking powder, baking soda and salt, then whisk together to combine.

Into the bowl of a stand mixer fitted with the paddle attachment, put the butter, sugar, maple syrup, vanilla and maple extract. Beat on medium-high until light and fluffy, 3 to 4 minutes. Add in the eggs, one at a time, beating well after each addition and scraping the sides of the bowl. Beat for an additional 2 minutes, or until the batter looks fluffy.

Add one-third of the dry ingredients to the stand mixer and mix on low until combined. Add half of the sour cream and mix on low until combined. Continue alternating the dry ingredients and the sour cream, until both have been completely added, finishing with the flour mixture. Fold in the chopped pecans.

Add half of the batter to the bottom of the Bundt pan. Sprinkle the pecan swirl mixture on top, then spoon the remaining batter over that and evenly spread it out with a spatula. Bake in the oven for 45 to 55 minutes, or until a toothpick comes out clean. Allow the cake to cool completely before glazing.

GLAZE

In a medium mixing bowl, combine all of the glaze ingredients and whisk together until smooth. Pipe or spoon onto the cooled Bundt cake.

Flavor-Stuffed
CREAM PUFFS & ÉCLAIRS

Éclairs and cream puffs have quickly made their way to the top of my favorite pastries list, and for good reason, too! The versatility of fillings makes these two sister pastries an amazing blank canvas that is ripe for flavor opportunities. In this chapter you will be delighted to find cream puffs and éclairs for a huge variety of palates: tiramisu for the coffee connoisseur (page 99), s'mores for the chocolate obsessed (page 103) and strawberry shortcake for those fruit lovers (page 97)! Who would have thought a simple dough made of flour, butter, milk, sugar and eggs could be the basis for so many wonderful creations!

SCRUMPTIOUS CHURRO ÉCLAIRS

I have a serious love affair with éclairs. They are my go-to pastry when I visit
patisseries or bakeries! I love the thin pastry shell, which is soft, yet almost slightly crisp.
And I really love whatever rich, velvety filling awaits within the borders of the pastry shell.
These perfectly puffed churro éclairs are covered in crunchy cinnamon-sugar coating and
filled with a luscious cinnamon dulce de leche pastry cream that will definitely rock
your world. It is best to make the dulce de leche pastry cream first or even the
day before. That way it has time to fully cool while you make everything else.

MAKES 10 ÉCLAIRS

DULCE DE LECHE
PASTRY CREAM

7 large egg yolks

1 cup plus 6 tbsp (330 ml) dulce
de leche

2¾ cups (660 ml) half-and-half

⅔ cup (160 ml) heavy cream

⅓ cup (43 g) cornstarch

3 tbsp (43 g) unsalted butter, at
room temperature

1 tbsp (15 ml) vanilla extract

1 tsp cinnamon

½ tsp table salt

CHOUX PASTRY

½ cup (120 ml) whole milk

½ cup (120 ml) water

½ cup (114 g) unsalted butter, at
room temperature

2 tsp (10 g) sugar

¾ tsp table salt

1 cup plus 3 tbsp (140 g)
all-purpose flour

4 large eggs plus 1 large egg,
for egg wash

1 to 2 tsp (5 to 10 ml) water,
for egg wash

DULCE DE LECHE PASTRY CREAM

In a medium saucepan, combine the egg yolks and dulce de leche.
Whisk until smooth. Add in the half-and-half, heavy cream and cornstarch. Whisk again until smooth.

Place the saucepan on the stove over medium heat. Cook the mixture,
whisking constantly, until it has thickened and just begins to bubble
(it should resemble the thickness of pudding). Once the pastry cream
is bubbling, continue to cook for exactly 1 minute, then remove from
the heat immediately.

Whisk in the butter, vanilla, cinnamon and salt, then place into a heatproof bowl. Place a piece of plastic wrap over the surface of the pastry
cream so a skin does not form, and place into the fridge to cool
completely, at least 4 hours, or preferably overnight.

CHOUX PASTRY

Preheat the oven to 475°F (245°C). Prepare two baking sheets by
lining them with parchment paper. Also prepare a pastry bag by
adding a round 1-inch (2.5-cm) tip.

In a medium saucepan over medium heat, combine the milk, water,
butter, sugar and salt and bring to a boil, stirring occasionally. Add
the flour into the pot all at once and begin to stir very quickly. A ball
of dough should form in almost no time. Continue cooking, stirring
constantly, for 4 to 5 minutes.

(continued)

CINNAMON-SUGAR COATING

½ cup (100 g) white sugar

1½ tsp (4 g) cinnamon

¼ cup (60 ml) unsalted butter, melted

Place the hot dough into the bowl of a stand mixer fitted with the paddle attachment and beat for 30 seconds to a minute to cool the dough down. Add one egg and beat until completely incorporated. Continue adding eggs one at a time, ensuring that each is completely incorporated before adding the next, scraping at the sides of the bowl occasionally.

After all the eggs are incorporated, transfer the dough to the piping bag and pipe it directly onto the parchment-lined baking sheets. Pipe ten 4-inch (10-cm)-long tubes, ensuring even piping pressure throughout. Crack the remaining egg into a bowl with the water and whisk them together to form an egg wash. Using a fork, brush the egg wash over the piped tubes, pressing slightly to create ridges.

Place the baking sheets in the oven, for exactly 1 minute, then immediately turn the oven off. After 9 minutes, turn the oven back on to 350°F (175°C) and bake for an additional 10 minutes. Rotate the pans and bake for another 10 minutes, or until the éclairs are puffed and golden (30 minutes total baking time). To ensure the éclairs are finished, remove one from the oven and check if it deflates within 45 seconds—if it deflates, they are not finished. In that case, place them back into the oven for 2 more minutes, then check again.

When the éclairs are finished, turn the oven off, and crack the oven one-third of the way open. Allow the éclairs to cool for 30 to 45 minutes in the open oven. Then, remove them and allow to cool completely before filling.

FILLING AND COATING WITH CINNAMON SUGAR

Transfer the dulce de leche pastry cream to a piping bag fitted with a small round piping tip. Poke the piping tip into one end of each éclair, then pipe the pastry cream into each one until it is full (you may have some leftover pastry cream depending on how much your éclairs puffed). Set the filled éclairs aside.

In a bowl, mix together the white sugar and cinnamon. Brush each éclair with the melted butter, then toss in the cinnamon sugar.

VELVETY COCONUT CREAM PIE ÉCLAIRS

These Coconut Cream Pie Éclairs are the definition of dreamy with their rich coconut milk pastry cream and strong coconut flavor that will be sure to transport you to the beaches of Hawaii! These éclairs are made from classic pâte à choux (choux pastry), topped with melted white chocolate and perfectly toasted shredded coconut. It is best to make the coconut pastry cream first or even the day before. That way it has time to fully cool while you make everything else!

MAKES 10 ÉCLAIRS

COCONUT PASTRY CREAM

7 large egg yolks

1 cup (200 g) white sugar

2 cups (480 ml) full-fat coconut milk, well mixed and smooth

1½ cups (360 ml) half-and-half

⅓ cup (43 g) cornstarch

2 tbsp (28 g) unsalted butter, at room temperature

2 tsp (10 ml) vanilla extract

¾ tsp coconut extract

½ tsp table salt

CHOUX PASTRY

½ cup (120 ml) whole milk

½ cup (120 ml) water

½ cup (114 g) unsalted butter, at room temperature

2 tsp (10 g) sugar

¾ tsp table salt

1 cup plus 3 tbsp (140 g) all-purpose flour

4 large eggs plus 1 large egg, for egg wash

1 to 2 tsp (5 to 10 ml) water, for egg wash

COCONUT PASTRY CREAM

In a medium saucepan, place the egg yolks and white sugar. Whisk until smooth. Add in the coconut milk, half-and-half and cornstarch. Whisk again until smooth.

Place the saucepan on the stove over medium heat. Cook the mixture, whisking constantly, until it has thickened and just begins to bubble (it should resemble the thickness of pudding). Once the pastry cream is bubbling, continue to cook for exactly 1 minute, then remove from the heat immediately.

Whisk in the butter, vanilla, coconut extract and salt, then transfer to a heatproof bowl. Place a piece of plastic wrap over the surface of the pastry cream so a skin does not form, and place the bowl into the fridge to cool completely, at least 4 hours, or preferably overnight.

CHOUX PASTRY

Preheat the oven to 475°F (245°C). Prepare two baking sheets by lining them with parchment paper. Also prepare a pastry bag by adding a round 1-inch (2.5-cm) tip.

In a medium saucepan over medium heat, combine the milk, water, butter, sugar and salt, then bring to a boil, stirring occasionally. Add the flour to the pot all at once, and begin to stir very quickly. A ball of dough should form in almost no time. Continue cooking, stirring constantly, for 4 to 5 minutes.

(continued)

TOPPING

1 cup (93 g) sweetened shredded coconut

8.8 oz (250 g) white chocolate, finely chopped

Place the hot dough into the bowl of a stand mixer fitted with the paddle attachment and beat for 30 seconds to a minute to cool the dough down. Add one egg and beat until completely incorporated. Continue adding eggs one at a time, ensuring that each is completely incorporated before adding the next, scraping at the sides of the bowl occasionally.

After all the eggs are incorporated, transfer the dough to the piping bag and pipe directly onto the parchment-lined baking sheets. Pipe ten 4-inch (10-cm)-long tubes, being careful to apply even piping pressure throughout. Crack the remaining egg into a bowl, add the water and whisk together to form an egg wash. Using a fork, brush the egg wash over the piped tubes, pressing slightly to create ridges.

Place the baking sheets into the 475°F (245°C) oven, for exactly 1 minute, then immediately turn the oven off. After 9 minutes, turn the oven back on to 350°F (175°C) and bake for an additional 10 minutes. Rotate pans and bake for another 10 minutes, or until the éclairs are puffed and golden (30 minutes total baking time). To ensure the éclairs are finished, remove one from the oven and check if it deflates within 45 seconds—if it deflates, they are not finished. In that case, place them back into the oven for 2 minutes, then check again.

When done, turn the oven off, and crack the oven one-third of the way open. Allow the éclairs to cool for 30 to 45 minutes in the open oven. Then, remove from the oven and allow to cool completely before filling.

FILLING AND TOPPING

Place a dry sauté pan on the stove over medium-high heat. Once the pan is hot, working in three batches, put the coconut in it. Toss and stir the coconut until it is all well-toasted and golden brown. Transfer the toasted coconut onto a plate to cool to room temperature and continue on to the next batch until all of the coconut has been toasted.

Transfer the cooled coconut pastry cream to a piping bag fitted with a small round piping tip. Poke the piping tip into one end of each éclair, then pipe the pastry cream into each one until it is full (you may have some leftover pastry cream depending on how much your éclairs puffed). Set the filled éclairs aside.

Add the chopped white chocolate to a microwave-proof bowl and place in the microwave for 1 to 2 minutes, or until melted (check at 1 minute, stir and heat again if needed). Dip the top of each filled éclair into the melted chocolate, then immediately sprinkle generously with toasted coconut. Place the assembled éclairs into the fridge to set for at least 1 hour.

SUMMERY STRAWBERRY SHORTCAKE CREAM PUFFS

This recipe is definitely one of my favorites in this book. Classic airy cream puffs are filled with juicy macerated strawberries and velvety whipped cream—the true meaning of simple yet delicious.

MAKES 16 CREAM PUFFS

CHOUX PASTRY

½ cup (120 ml) whole milk

½ cup (120 ml) water

½ cup (114 g) unsalted butter, at room temperature

1 tbsp (15 g) sugar

1 tsp table salt

1 cup (125 g) all-purpose flour

4 large eggs plus 1 large egg, for egg wash

1 to 2 tsp (5 to 10 ml) water, for egg wash

CHOUX PASTRY

Preheat the oven to 475°F (245°C). Prepare two baking sheets by lining them with parchment paper. Also prepare a pastry bag by adding a round 1-inch (2.5-cm) tip.

In a medium saucepan over medium heat, combine the milk, water, butter, sugar and salt and bring to a boil, stirring occasionally. Add the flour to the pot all at once, and begin to stir very quickly. A ball of dough should form in almost no time. Continue cooking, stirring constantly, for 1 minute.

Place the hot dough into the bowl of a stand mixer fitted with the paddle attachment and beat for 30 seconds to a minute, to cool the dough down. Add one egg and beat until completely incorporated. Continue adding eggs one at a time, ensuring that each is completely incorporated before adding the next, scraping down the sides of the bowl occasionally.

After all the eggs are incorporated, transfer the dough to the piping bag and pipe directly onto the parchment-lined baking sheets. Pipe about eight 2-inch (5-cm)-wide rounds per baking sheet (about 16 total). Crack the remaining egg into a bowl with the water and whisk together to form an egg wash. Brush the egg wash over the piped cream puffs. Use a wet finger to press down any peaks or bumps.

Place into the 475°F (245°C) oven, for exactly 1 minute, then immediately turn the oven off. After 9 minutes, turn the oven back on to 350°F (175°C) and bake for an additional 10 minutes. Rotate the pans and bake for another 10 minutes, or until the cream puffs are puffed and golden (30 minutes total baking time). To ensure the cream puffs are finished, remove one from the oven and check if it deflates within 45 seconds—if it deflates, they are not finished. If this happens, place them back in the oven for 2 minutes, then check again.

(continued)

FILLING

1 lb (454 g) strawberries, hulled and sliced

2 tbsp (30 g) white sugar

2½ cups (600 ml) heavy cream, chilled

½ cup (60 g) confectioners' sugar

When done, turn the oven off, and crack the oven a third of the way open. Allow the cream puffs to cool for 30 to 45 minutes in the open oven. Then, remove them from the oven and allow to cool completely before filling.

FILLING AND ASSEMBLING

Put the sliced strawberries into a bowl, then top with white sugar and toss. Allow the strawberries to sit and macerate for 15 minutes.

Put the cream and confectioners' sugar into the bowl of a stand mixer or mixing bowl, then beat on medium-high until stiff peaks form.

Using a serrated knife, cut off the top of each cream puff. Using a spoon or a piping bag fitted with a star tip, fill the bottom of each cream puff with whipped cream, place some macerated strawberries on top, spoon in some juice from the macerated strawberries, then top with more whipped cream. Place the top back on and enjoy immediately or keep in the fridge until ready to serve.

COFFEE LOVERS' TIRAMISU CREAM PUFFS

This hybrid dessert of the almighty cream puff and my favorite dessert, tiramisu, is truly a dessert lover's dream! This recipe features a brown sugar craquelin–crusted cream puff that is piped full of a silky smooth chocolate coffee filling. Chocolatey, rich and creamy, these little cream puffs are heavenly. It is best to make the coffee ganache filling first, that way it has time to fully cool while you make everything else.

MAKES 16 CREAM PUFFS

CREAMY COFFEE GANACHE FILLING

7 oz (198 g) semi-sweet chocolate, finely chopped

3 cups (720 ml) heavy cream

½ cup (100 g) white sugar

6 tbsp (90 ml) Kahlúa

2½ tsp (5 g) instant coffee powder

2 cups (464 g) mascarpone cheese

CRAQUELIN TOPPING

1 cup (125 g) all-purpose flour

½ cup (110 g) dark brown sugar

7 tbsp (99 g) unsalted butter, softened

CREAMY COFFEE GANACHE FILLING

Put the chopped chocolate into a heatproof bowl and set aside.

In a medium saucepan over medium heat, combine the cream, sugar, Kahlúa and coffee powder. Bring to a simmer, then remove from the heat and pour the mixture over the chopped chocolate. Stir the mixture lightly with a rubber spatula, then allow it to sit for 3 minutes to allow the chocolate to melt. After 3 minutes, whisk the ganache until it comes together and is smooth.

Wrap the bowl with plastic wrap, then put it in the fridge for at least 6 hours, or preferably overnight.

CRAQUELIN TOPPING

Put all of the craquelin ingredients in a medium-sized bowl, then mash them together with a spatula or your fingers until a uniform-looking dough forms.

Place the dough between two pieces of parchment paper, then roll it out to be about ⅛ inch (3 mm) thick (try to make it into a perfect rectangle, as it makes cutting out the circles easier later). Place into the freezer for at least 30 minutes while you make the choux.

(continued)

CHOUX PASTRY

½ cup (120 ml) whole milk

½ cup (120 ml) water

½ cup (114 g) unsalted butter, at room temperature

1 tbsp (15 g) sugar

1 tsp table salt

1 cup (125 g) all-purpose flour

4 large eggs

CHOUX PASTRY

Preheat the oven to 475°F (245°C). Prepare two baking sheets by lining them with parchment paper. Also prepare a pastry bag by adding a round 1-inch (2.5-cm) tip.

In a medium saucepan over medium heat, combine the milk, water, butter, sugar and salt and bring to a boil, stirring occasionally. Add the flour to the pot all at once, and begin to stir very quickly. A ball of dough should form in almost no time. Continue cooking, stirring constantly, for 1 minute.

Place the hot dough into a stand mixer fitted with the paddle attachment and beat for 30 seconds to a minute, to cool the dough down. Add one egg and beat until completely incorporated. Continue adding eggs one at a time, ensuring that each is completely incorporated before adding the next, scraping down the sides of the bowl occasionally.

After all the eggs are incorporated, transfer the dough to the piping bag and pipe directly onto parchment-lined baking sheets. Pipe about eight 2-inch (5-cm)-wide rounds per baking sheet (about 16 total). Cut 16 rounds out of the cold craquelin topping, each about the same diameter as the piped cream puffs. Place each round onto a piped cream puff, lightly pressing it down to secure it.

Place the baking sheets into the oven, for exactly 1 minute, then immediately turn the oven off. After 9 minutes, turn the oven back on to 350°F (175°C) and bake for an additional 10 minutes. Rotate the pans and bake for another 10 minutes, or until the cream puffs are puffed and golden (30 minutes total baking time). To ensure the cream puffs are finished, remove one from the oven and check if it deflates within 45 seconds—if it deflates, they are not finished. If that happens, place them back into the oven for 2 minutes, then check again.

When done, turn the oven off, and crack the oven a third of the way open. Allow the cream puffs to cool for 30 to 45 minutes in the cracked oven. Then, remove them from the oven and allow to cool completely before filling.

FINISHING THE FILLING AND ASSEMBLING

When the ganache is cold, remove it from the fridge and transfer it to a stand mixer fitted with the whisk attachment. Beat on high until fluffy. Add in the mascarpone cheese, then beat again until the mascarpone is fully incorporated.

Transfer the filling into a piping bag fitted with a small round tip. Puncture the bottom of each cream puff and pipe the filling in until the cream puff is full. Enjoy immediately or keep in the fridge.

"EVERYTHING BUT THE TENT" S'MORES CREAM PUFFS

Covered in a crunchy brown sugar craquelin topping and filled with a silky whipped chocolate ganache and toasted marshmallow filling, these cream puffs bring together all the classic s'mores flavors we all know and love from our childhood! It is best to make the chocolate ganache filling first, that way it has time to fully cool while you make everything else.

MAKES 16 CREAM PUFFS

WHIPPED CHOCOLATE GANACHE
12 oz (338 g) semisweet chocolate, finely chopped
3 cups (720 ml) heavy cream

CRAQUELIN TOPPING
1 cup (125 g) all-purpose flour
½ cup (110 g) dark brown sugar
7 tbsp (99 g) unsalted butter, softened

WHIPPED CHOCOLATE GANACHE

Put the chopped chocolate into a heatproof bowl and set aside.

Pour the cream into a medium saucepan over medium heat. Bring to a simmer, then remove it from the heat and pour over the chopped chocolate. Stir the mixture lightly with a rubber spatula, then let it sit for 3 minutes to allow the chocolate to melt. After 3 minutes, whisk the ganache until it comes together and is smooth.

Wrap the bowl with plastic wrap, then place it into the fridge for at least 6 hours, or preferably overnight.

CRAQUELIN TOPPING

In a medium-sized bowl, combine all of the craquelin ingredients, then mash them together with a spatula or your fingers until a uniform-looking dough forms.

Place the dough between two pieces of parchment paper, then roll the dough out to be about ⅛ inch (3 mm) thick (try to make it into a perfect rectangle, as it makes cutting out the circles easier later). Place into the freezer for at least 30 minutes, while you make the choux.

(continued)

CHOUX PASTRY

½ cup (120 ml) whole milk

½ cup (120 ml) water

½ cup (114 g) unsalted butter, at room temperature

1 tbsp (15 g) sugar

1 tsp table salt

1 cup (125 g) all-purpose flour

4 large eggs

CHOUX PASTRY

Preheat the oven to 475°F (245°C). Prepare two baking sheets by lining them with parchment paper. Also prepare a pastry bag by adding a round 1-inch (2.5-cm) tip.

In a medium saucepan over medium heat, combine the milk, water, butter, sugar and salt and bring to a boil, stirring occasionally. Add the flour into the pot all at once, and begin to stir very quickly. A ball of dough should form in almost no time. Continue cooking, stirring constantly, for 1 minute.

Place the hot dough into a stand mixer fitted with the paddle attachment, and beat for 30 seconds to a minute, to cool the dough down. Add one egg and beat until completely incorporated. Continue adding eggs one at a time ensuring that each is completely incorporated before adding the next, scraping down the sides of the bowl occasionally.

After all the eggs are incorporated, transfer the dough to the piping bag and pipe directly onto parchment-lined baking sheets. Pipe about eight 2-inch (5-cm)-wide rounds per baking sheet (about 16 total). Cut out 16 rounds out of the cold craquelin topping, about the same diameter as the piped cream puffs. Place each round onto a piped cream puff, lightly pressing it down to secure it.

Place the baking sheets into the oven, for exactly 1 minute, then immediately turn the oven off. After 9 minutes, turn the oven back on to 350°F (175°C) and bake for an additional 10 minutes. Rotate the pans and bake for another 10 minutes, or until the cream puffs are puffed and golden (30 minutes total baking time). To ensure the cream puffs are finished, remove one from the oven and check if it deflates within 45 seconds—if it deflates they are not finished. If that happens, place them back into the oven for 2 minutes, then check again.

When done, turn the oven off, and crack the oven a third of the way open. Allow the cream puffs to cool for 30 to 45 minutes in the cracked oven. Then, remove them from the oven and allow to cool completely before filling.

MARSHMALLOW FILLING
⅔ cup (160 g) fresh egg whites
1¼ cups (250 g) white sugar
1 tsp vanilla extract

MARSHMALLOW FILLING

In the bowl of a stand mixer, combine the egg whites and sugar, and whisk together. Set the bowl over the top of a simmering pot of water, making sure that a tight seal forms and that the bottom of the stand mixer bowl is not actually touching the water.

Continuously whisk the mixture by hand while it heats up over the simmering water, heating it until it reaches 160°F (71°C) on a kitchen thermometer. When this temperature is reached, remove the bowl from the simmering water pot and put it onto your stand mixer. Using the whisk attachment, beat the mixture on high for 4 to 5 minutes or until very stiff, glossy peaks are achieved. Add the vanilla, then beat for 10 more seconds to incorporate. Transfer the meringue to a piping bag fitted with a closed star tip.

FILLING AND ASSEMBLING

When the ganache is cold, remove it from the fridge and transfer it to a stand mixer fitted with the whisk attachment. Beat on high until fluffy.

Using a serrated knife, cut off the top of each cream puff. Spoon the whipped chocolate ganache into the bottom of each cream puff, then pipe the marshmallow filling over the top of that. Torch the marsh-mallow topping with a kitchen torch. Place the top back on and enjoy immediately, or keep in the fridge until ready to serve.

Cheat Day-Style

DONUTS

Dusted with cinnamon sugar, stuffed with coconut pastry cream or covered with a rich chocolate glaze, the donuts in this section can only be described as downright delicious! In this chapter you will find all kinds of variations of donuts, both baked and fried, that are perfect for cheat days. From Silky Pumpkin Cream–Filled Donuts (page 110) to petite donut holes jam-packed with dulce de leche (page 116), this chapter is sure to satisfy any donut craving.

CHOCOLATE-GLAZED BANANA BREAD BAKED DONUTS

This banana bread–donut hybrid has a tender and moist crumb that is an absolute delight to eat. Overripe bananas are the key to making these ultra flavorful with that melt-in-your-mouth moistness. A rich chocolate glaze and crushed pecans are decadent finishing touches that further elevate these donuts.

MAKES 18 DONUTS

BANANA BREAD DONUTS

1 cup (220 g) packed dark brown sugar

½ cup (120 ml) sour cream

¼ cup (60 ml) unsalted butter, melted

¼ cup (60 ml) vegetable oil

3 medium overripe bananas, mashed smooth

2 large eggs

1 tsp vanilla extract

1¾ cups (210 g) all-purpose flour

1 tsp baking soda

½ tsp table salt

½ tsp cinnamon

CHOCOLATE GLAZE

6.3 oz (180 g) semisweet chocolate, finely chopped

3 tbsp (42 g) coconut oil

¼ cup (27 g) crushed pecans

BANANA BREAD DONUTS

Preheat the oven to 350°F (175°C). Prepare three donut pans (18 donuts total) with baking or cooking spray. In a large mixing bowl, combine the brown sugar, sour cream, melted butter, vegetable oil, mashed bananas, eggs and vanilla. Whisk together until very smooth and combined.

In a separate mixing bowl, whisk together the flour, baking soda, salt and cinnamon until well combined. Pour these dry ingredients into the wet ingredients, then whisk together just until a smooth batter comes together.

Transfer the batter to a piping bag with a wide tip and pipe it evenly into the donut cavities, filling each about halfway full, then tap each pan lightly to even out the batter. Place the pans into the oven to bake for 11 to 12 minutes, or until an inserted toothpick comes out clean.

Allow the donuts to cool in the pan for 10 minutes, then transfer to a rack to finish cooling to room temperature, about 2 hours.

CHOCOLATE GLAZE

Combine the chopped chocolate and coconut oil in a heatproof bowl and place over a pot of simmering water, making sure the bowl fits tightly over the pot of water and that the bottom does not touch the water. Heat while stirring with a rubber spatula, until all of the chocolate has melted and the coconut oil is mixed in. Allow it to cool for 5 minutes.

Dip the top of each donut into the chocolate glaze, then top immediately with crushed pecans. Place the donuts into the fridge to set for 30 minutes to 1 hour.

SILKY PUMPKIN CREAM-FILLED DONUTS

There is nothing quite like a homemade donut. I've always loved the taste of the sweet, yeasty dough that has been fried up to golden perfection. These donuts are soft and pillowy in texture and filled with a luscious pumpkin pastry cream. The flavor brings back nostalgic Thanksgiving memories! It is best to make the pumpkin pastry cream first or even the day before. That way it has time to fully cool while you make everything else!

MAKES 10 DONUTS

PUMPKIN PASTRY CREAM

5 large egg yolks

⅔ cup (132 g) white sugar

½ cup (110 g) packed brown sugar

1 cup (245 g) pumpkin purée

1 cup (240 ml) half-and-half

1 cup (240 ml) heavy cream

¼ cup (32 g) cornstarch

1 tsp cinnamon

1 tsp allspice

2 tbsp (28 g) unsalted butter, at room temperature

1½ tsp (8 ml) vanilla extract

¼ tsp table salt

DONUTS

6 tbsp (90 ml) water, warmed

⅔ cup buttermilk (160 ml), at room temperature

¼ cup (60 ml) unsalted butter, melted

¼ cup (50 g) white sugar

1¾ tsp (6 g) instant yeast

1 large egg, lightly beaten, at room temperature

3¾ cups (454 g) all-purpose flour

1 tsp table salt

Shortening or oil for frying

PUMPKIN PASTRY CREAM

In a medium saucepan, combine the egg yolks, white sugar and brown sugar. Whisk until smooth. Add in the pumpkin purée, half-and-half, heavy cream, cornstarch, cinnamon and allspice. Whisk again until smooth.

Place the saucepan on the stove over medium heat. Cook the mixture, whisking constantly, until it has thickened and just begins to bubble (it should resemble the thickness of pudding). Once the pastry cream is bubbling, continue to cook it for exactly 1 minute, then remove it from the heat immediately.

Add in the butter, vanilla and salt, then place into a heatproof bowl. Place a piece of plastic wrap over the surface of the pastry cream so a skin does not form, and place it into the fridge to cool completely, at least 4 hours, or preferably overnight.

DONUTS

In the bowl of a stand mixer fitted with the dough hook, combine the water, buttermilk, melted butter, sugar, yeast and egg. Whisk together to combine.

In a small mixing bowl, whisk together the flour and salt. Add the dry ingredients to the stand mixer bowl, then using a large wooden spoon, mix together until a shaggy dough forms. Turn the stand mixer on to medium. Beat the dough for about 8 minutes, or until the dough is smooth, elastic and tacky.

Transfer the dough to a large greased bowl, cover with plastic wrap, then place it in a warm area to rise for about 2 hours, or until the dough is doubled in size.

(continued)

CINNAMON-SUGAR COATING

1 cup (200 g) white sugar

1 tbsp (8 g) cinnamon

While the dough proofs, cut out 10 parchment squares that are at least 4 x 4 inches (10 x 10 cm). Place these parchment squares onto two baking sheets.

When the dough is proofed, punch it down, then divide it into 10 equal-sized pieces. Roll each piece into a round, smooth ball. Transfer the dough balls onto the individual parchment squares on the baking sheets.

Place the baking sheets into a warm, humid area to let the dough rise for 20 to 30 minutes, or until doubled in size. The best way to do this is by placing the baking sheets with dough onto the top and middle racks of your oven, then placing an empty baking sheet onto the bottom rack and filling that with boiling water. Close the oven, then turn it on to 350°F (175°C) for exactly one minute, then immediately turn it off (do not let the oven actually reach 350°F [175°C], you are only turning the oven on for 1 minute to slightly warm the oven to encourage rising). Alternatively, if your oven has a "bread proof" function, just turn that on instead.

CINNAMON-SUGAR COATING

Meanwhile, make the cinnamon-sugar coating by whisking together the white sugar and cinnamon in a medium mixing bowl. Set aside.

FRYING AND FILLING THE DONUTS

Add the oil to a large, wide pot, such as a Dutch oven, filling it about halfway. Heat the oil over medium-high heat until it reaches between 350 to 375°F (175 to 190°C) on a kitchen thermometer. When ready, carefully pick up the donuts along with the parchment, and place them into the hot oil. Fish out the parchment squares and fry the donuts for about 1½ minutes per side, or until golden brown. Remove the donuts with tongs or a spider, then place them onto a paper towel–lined baking sheet. While the donuts are still quite warm, toss them in the cinnamon sugar, then place them on a rack to cool to room temperature before filling, 2 to 3 hours.

Once cooled, insert a bamboo skewer about halfway into each donut, then wiggle it around to create a pocket for the filling. Transfer the pumpkin pastry cream to a piping bag fitted with a small round piping tip. Poke the piping tip into the hole, then pipe the pastry cream into each donut until it is full.

TROPICAL COCONUT CREAM PIE DONUTS

One word to describe these donuts? Dreamy. Seriously dreaaaaamy. These donuts are fluffy and soft, filled with a smooth coconut pastry cream, and dusted generously with confectioners' sugar. It is best to make the coconut pastry cream first or even the day before. That way it has time to fully cool while you make everything else!

MAKES 10 DONUTS

COCONUT PASTRY CREAM

5 large egg yolks

1 cup (200 g) white sugar

1½ cups (360 ml) full-fat coconut milk, well mixed to be smooth

1 cup (240 ml) half-and-half

¼ cup (32 g) cornstarch

1 tbsp (14 g) unsalted butter, at room temperature

1½ tsp (7.5 ml) vanilla extract

½ tsp coconut extract

¼ tsp table salt

DONUTS

6 tbsp (90 ml) water, warmed

⅔ cup buttermilk (160 ml), at room temperature

¼ cup (60 ml) unsalted butter, melted

¼ cup (50 g) white sugar

1¾ tsp (6 g) instant yeast

1 large egg, lightly beaten, at room temperature

3¾ cups (454 g) all-purpose flour

1 tsp table salt

Shortening or oil for frying

¼ cup (30 g) confectioners' sugar, for dusting on top

COCONUT PASTRY CREAM

In a medium saucepan, combine the egg yolks and white sugar. Whisk until smooth. Add in the coconut milk, half-and-half and cornstarch. Whisk again until smooth.

Place the saucepan on the stove over medium heat. Cook the mixture, whisking constantly, until the mixture has thickened and just begins to bubble (it should resemble the thickness of pudding). Once the pastry cream is bubbling, continue to cook for exactly 1 minute, then remove from the heat immediately.

Add in the butter, vanilla, coconut extract and salt, then transfer to a heatproof bowl. Place a piece of plastic wrap over the surface of the pastry cream so a skin does not form, and place into the fridge to cool completely, at least 4 hours, or preferably overnight.

DONUTS

In the bowl of a stand mixer, combine the water, buttermilk, melted butter, sugar, yeast and egg. Whisk together by hand to combine.

In a small mixing bowl, whisk together the flour and salt. Add to the stand mixer bowl. Then, using a large wooden spoon, mix together until a shaggy dough forms. Fit the stand mixer with the dough hook, put the mixer bowl onto the machine and turn the mixer onto medium. Beat the dough for about 8 minutes, or until the dough is smooth, elastic and tacky.

Transfer the dough to a large greased bowl, cover with plastic wrap, then place in a warm area to rise for about 2 hours, or until the dough is doubled in size.

While the dough proofs, cut out 10 parchment squares that are at least 4 x 4 inches (10 x 10 cm). Place these parchment squares onto two baking sheets.

(continued)

When the dough is proofed, punch the dough down, then divide into 10 equal-sized pieces. Roll each piece into a round smooth ball. Transfer the dough balls onto the individual parchment squares on the baking sheets.

Place the baking sheets into a warm, humid area to let the dough rise for 20 to 30 minutes, or until doubled in size. The best way to do this is by placing the baking sheets with the dough onto the top and middle racks of your oven, then placing an empty baking sheet onto the bottom rack and filling that baking sheet with boiling water. Close the oven, then turn it on to 350°F (175°C) for exactly 1 minute, then immediately turn it off (do not let the oven actually reach 350°F [175°C], you are only turning the oven on for 1 minute to slightly warm the oven to encourage rising). Alternatively, if your oven has a "bread proof" function, turn that on instead.

Meanwhile, add the oil to a large wide pot, such as a Dutch oven, filling it about halfway. Heat the oil over medium-high heat until it reaches between 350 to 375°F (175 to 190°C) on a kitchen thermometer. When ready, carefully pick up the donuts with the parchment, and place them into the hot oil. Fish out the parchment squares and fry the donuts for about 1½ minutes per side, or until golden brown. Remove donuts with tongs or a spider, then place them onto a paper towel–lined baking sheet to cool to room temperature, 2 or 3 hours.

FILLING AND ASSEMBLY

Insert a bamboo skewer about halfway into each donut, then wiggle it around to create a pocket for the filling. Transfer the coconut pastry cream to a piping bag fitted with a small round piping tip. Poke the piping tip into the hole, then pipe the pastry cream into each donut until it is full. Finish by dusting the donuts with confectioners' sugar.

DULCE-STUFFED CHURRO DONUT HOLES

Can you guess what my favorite thing about making donuts is? It's the leftover donut holes, of course! I love the bite-sized balls of sweet, yeasty bread that you can quickly just pop into your mouth and enjoy. Therefore, it was a no-brainer for me to include a full-blown donut hole recipe in the book! These churro-inspired donut holes are coated in sweet cinnamon sugar and then piped full of deeply rich dulce de leche!

MAKES 25 TO 30 DONUT HOLES

CHURRO DONUT HOLES
6 tbsp (90 ml) water, warmed

⅔ cup (160 ml) buttermilk, at room temperature

¼ cup (60 ml) unsalted butter, melted

¼ cup (50 g) white sugar

1¾ tsp (5 g) instant yeast

1 large egg, lightly beaten, at room temperature

3¾ cups (454 g) all-purpose flour, plus more for dusting

1 tsp table salt

Shortening or oil for frying

CINNAMON-SUGAR COATING AND DULCE DE LECHE FILLING
½ cup (100 g) white sugar

2 tsp (5 g) cinnamon

1 cup (240 ml) dulce de leche, for filling

In the bowl of a stand mixer, whisk the water, buttermilk, melted butter, sugar, yeast and egg by hand to combine.

In a small mixing bowl, whisk together the flour and salt. Add to the stand mixer bowl. Then, using a large wooden spoon, mix together until a shaggy dough forms. Fit the stand mixer with the dough hook, put the bowl on the mixer and turn the mixer on to medium. Beat the dough for about 8 minutes, or until the dough is smooth, elastic and tacky.

Transfer the dough to a large greased bowl, cover with plastic wrap, then place in a warm area to rise for about 2 hours, or until the dough is doubled in size.

Just before the dough is properly proofed, add the frying oil to a large wide pot, such as a Dutch oven, filling it about halfway. Heat the oil over medium-high heat until it reaches between 350 to 375°F (175 to 190°C) on a kitchen thermometer. Make the cinnamon-sugar coating by whisking together the white sugar and cinnamon in a medium mixing bowl. Set aside.

Turn the proofed dough out onto a lightly floured work surface and roll out to be about ½ inch (1.3 cm) thick. Using a 2¼-inch (6-cm) cookie cutter, cut out donut holes. Working in batches, place the donut holes into the hot oil. Fry the donut holes for 1 to 2 minutes per side, or until golden brown. Remove the donut holes with tongs or a spider, then place onto a paper towel–lined baking sheet. While the donuts are still quite warm, toss them in the cinnamon sugar, then place them on a rack to cool for at least an hour.

When the donut holes have cooled, transfer the dulce de leche into a piping bag fitted with a small- to medium-sized round tip. Insert a bamboo skewer about halfway into each donut hole, then lightly wiggle it around to create a small pocket for the filling. Insert the piping bag tip and squeeze the dulce de leche into each donut hole. These are best served the same day.

Blissfully Delicious
CHEESECAKES & PAVLOVAS

If there are any desserts that truly seem heaven-sent, it would have to be cheesecakes and pavlovas! They are obviously both delicious in their own right—cheesecake with its luscious, velvety texture and pavlovas with their delectably crisp exteriors and pillowy soft interiors. But what makes them even greater is their adaptability and capacity to take on any flavor profile and topping! Throughout this chapter, you'll be introduced to some truly decadent cheesecakes and pavlovas that are not only sensationally delicious, but could be considered showstopping dessert "art" as well!

HEAVENLY BANANA CREAM PIE PAVLOVA

Silky banana pudding, fluffy whipped cream, sliced banana rounds and a sizeable drizzling of salted caramel, all on top of a cloudy, dream-like pavlova. Life = complete. This pavlova is made with boxed banana pudding to create that classic banana cream pie flavor. To make a perfect pavlova, it is best to make it in the evening, then leave it in the oven to cool overnight. And remember, resist the urge to peek, even when it's cooling!

Note: As pavlovas can be quite finicky and sensitive to variances in the measurements, I highly recommend that you use a kitchen scale and measure the ingredients using the weight (grams) given, rather than going by volume.

MAKES 1 (8-INCH [20-CM]) PAVLOVA

PAVLOVA

200 g (13 tbsp plus 1 tsp) fresh egg whites

350 g (1¾ cups) white sugar

5 g (2 tsp) cornstarch

10 ml (2 tsp) white vinegar

1 tsp vanilla extract

PAVLOVA

Preheat the oven to 330°F (165°C). Prepare a large baking sheet with parchment. Draw an 8-inch (20-cm) circle on the center of the parchment.

In the bowl of your stand mixer, combine the egg whites and sugar, and whisk together. Set the bowl over the top of a simmering pot of water, making sure a tight seal forms and that the bottom of the stand mixer bowl is not actually touching the water.

Continuously whisk the mixture by hand while it heats up over the simmering water, heating it until it reaches 165 to 170°F (74 to 77°C) on a kitchen thermometer. When that temperature is reached, remove the bowl from the simmering water pot and place it onto your stand mixer. Using the whisk attachment, beat the mixture on high for 4 to 5 minutes or until very stiff, glossy peaks are achieved.

Turn the stand mixer off and add in the cornstarch, vinegar and vanilla. Turn the stand mixer back on high for 10 seconds to mix everything together.

Place a small amount of the meringue onto each of the corners of the parchment paper to secure it to the baking sheet. Place the meringue in the center of the parchment. Using the circle as a guide, spread and smooth the meringue with a spatula from the center outward, creating an 8-inch (20-cm)-wide disk that is slightly thicker around the edges and has a ½-inch (1.3-cm) depression in the center.

(continued)

SALTED CARAMEL

½ cup (100 g) white sugar

2 tbsp (30 ml) water

3 tbsp (42 g) unsalted butter, at room temperature and cubed

¼ cup (60 ml) heavy cream

½ tsp vanilla extract

½ tsp table salt

TOPPING

1 cup (240 ml) banana pudding from a box

½ cup (120 ml) heavy cream

½ tbsp (4 g) confectioners' sugar

1 or 2 bananas, sliced

Place the pavlova into the oven, then immediately turn the oven down to 220°F (105°C). Bake for 2 hours. After 2 hours, turn off the oven (do not open the oven) and allow the pavlova to cool there for at least 4 hours or very preferably overnight.

SALTED CARAMEL

In a large saucepan over medium heat, mix together the sugar and water. Stir occasionally until the sugar has dissolved and the mixture begins to boil.

Once the mixture begins to boil, turn the heat up to medium-high and allow the mixture to continue to boil, being careful not to stir it, until it turns amber in color (stirring the mixture will cause crystallization, so refrain from stirring).

Once the mixture has become amber in color (360°F [182°C] on a candy thermometer), add the cubed butter and mix very vigorously to combine. (Be careful, however, because the mixture will bubble and rise up rapidly when you add the butter.) If the butter seems to be separating from the caramel, remove it from the heat, then whisk vigorously until it comes together.

Next, slowly drizzle in the heavy cream (it will bubble rapidly again) while whisking. Then add the vanilla and salt. Whisk until smooth and well combined. Remove the caramel from the heat, then set aside to cool to room temperature.

TOPPING

Prepare the banana pudding according to the box directions, then place into the fridge with plastic wrap over the surface to cool completely.

At serving time, put the heavy cream and confectioners' sugar in a stand mixer or mixing bowl, then beat on medium-high until stiff peaks form.

Top the pavlova with 1 cup (240 ml) of the banana pudding. Then top with the whipped cream, salted caramel and sliced bananas.

DELICIOUSLY DIVINE BLACK FOREST PAVLOVA

Jammy, sweet cherry compote and chocolate-infused whipped cream over the top of a dessert with a cloudy marshmallow interior and crisp exterior. Sounds fan-freaking-tastic, right? This pavlova is a definite showstopper of a dessert, both visually and flavor-wise! To make a perfect pavlova, it is best to make it in the evening and leave it in the oven to cool overnight. And remember, resist the urge to peek, even when it's cooling!
Note: As pavlovas can be quite finicky and sensitive to variances in the measurements, I highly recommend that you use a kitchen scale and measure the ingredients using the weight (grams) given, rather than going by volume.

MAKES 1 (8-INCH [20-CM]) PAVLOVA

PAVLOVA

200 g (13 tbsp plus 1 tsp) fresh egg whites
350 g (1¾ cups) white sugar
5 g (2 tsp) cornstarch
10 ml (2 tsp) white vinegar
1 tsp vanilla extract

PAVLOVA

Preheat the oven to 330°F (165°C). Prepare a large baking sheet with parchment. Draw an 8-inch (20-cm) circle on the center of the parchment.

In the bowl of a stand mixer, combine the egg whites and sugar and whisk together. Set the bowl over the top of a simmering pot of water, making sure a tight seal forms and that the bottom of the stand mixer bowl is not actually touching the water.

Continuously whisk the mixture by hand while it heats up over the simmering water, until it reaches 165 to 170°F (74 to 77°C) on a kitchen thermometer. When this temperature is reached, remove the bowl from the simmering water pot and place it onto your stand mixer. Using the whisk attachment, beat the mixture on high for 4 to 5 minutes or until very stiff, glossy peaks are achieved.

Turn the stand mixer off and add the cornstarch, vinegar and vanilla to the meringue. Turn the stand mixer back on high for 10 seconds to mix everything together.

Place a small amount of meringue onto each of the corners of the parchment paper to secure it to the baking sheet. Place the meringue in the center of the parchment. Using the circle as a guide, spread and smooth the meringue with a spatula from the center outward, creating an 8-inch (20-cm)-wide disk that is slightly thicker around the edges and has a ½-inch (1.3-cm) depression in the center.

Place the pavlova into the oven, then immediately turn the oven down to 220°F (105°C). Bake for 2 hours. After 2 hours, turn off the oven (do not open the oven) and allow the pavlova to cool in the oven for at least 4 hours or very preferably overnight.

(continued)

CHERRY COMPOTE

1 lb (454 g) frozen cherries, thawed

2 tbsp (30 g) white sugar

Juice of ½ lemon

1 tbsp (15 ml) kirsch cherry liqueur (optional)

Fresh black cherries, for garnish (optional)

CHOCOLATE WHIPPED CREAM

1½ cups (360 ml) heavy cream

5.3 oz (150 g) dark chocolate or semi-sweet chocolate, finely chopped

CHERRY COMPOTE

In a medium saucepan over medium-high heat, combine the thawed cherries and sugar. Bring to a boil, then reduce the heat to medium and allow the compote to simmer until thick and syrupy—15 to 20 minutes.

Remove the compote from the heat, stir in the lemon juice and kirsch, if using, and place into a heatproof container and set into the fridge to cool completely, 3 to 4 hours.

CHOCOLATE WHIPPED CREAM

Pour the heavy cream into a small saucepan over medium heat. Bring it to a simmer, then immediately remove it from the heat.

Put the chopped chocolate in a heatproof medium mixing bowl, then pour the hot cream over it. Stir lightly with a spatula, then let the mixture sit for 3 minutes to melt the chocolate. After 3 minutes, whisk the ganache together until incorporated and smooth.

Cover the ganache with plastic wrap, then place it into the fridge to cool for at least 3 to 4 hours, or preferably overnight.

When the ganache is cold, remove it from the fridge and transfer it to a stand mixer fitted with the whisk attachment. Beat on high until fluffy.

ASSEMBLY

Place the pavlova onto the desired serving platter, then top it with cooled cherry compote and chocolate whipped cream. Finish with fresh black cherries, if desired.

DOWNRIGHT DREAMY COCONUT CREAM CHEESECAKE

This coconut cream cheesecake, with its rich tropical cheesecake base and crumbly graham cracker crust, is truly the epitome of delicious. This cheesecake is velvety and rich in texture, and is filled with tons of coconut flavor thanks to the coconut milk, coconut extract and the whipped coconut topping! A true tropical delight.

MAKES 1 (9-INCH [23-CM]) CHEESECAKE

GRAHAM CRACKER CRUST

2¼ cups (300 g) graham cracker crumbs

⅓ cup (66 g) white sugar

10 tbsp (150 ml) unsalted butter, melted

COCONUT CHEESECAKE

4 (8-oz [226-g]) blocks cream cheese, well softened

1½ cups (300 g) white sugar

2¼ tsp (11 ml) coconut extract

1 tsp vanilla extract

¼ tsp table salt

3 large eggs, at room temperature

2 large egg yolks, at room temperature

1 cup (240 ml) full-fat canned coconut milk, well mixed

½ cup (120 ml) sour cream

1 tbsp (8 g) cornstarch

GRAHAM CRACKER CRUST

Preheat the oven to 350°F (175°C). In a bowl, combine the graham cracker crumbs and sugar and whisk together. Pour the melted butter into the bowl, then mix with a fork or your hands until the butter is well dispersed and the mixture resembles wet sand.

Grease a 9- or 10-inch (23- or 25-cm) springform pan, then put the crust into the pan and press it down evenly into the bottom and halfway up the sides. Use a flat-bottomed measuring cup to really compact the crust. Put the crust in the oven to bake for 10 minutes. Remove from the oven and allow to cool to room temperature.

COCONUT CHEESECAKE

Turn the oven down to 325°F (160°C). Prepare the cooled springform pan (with the crust) by wrapping the bottom of the pan with two sheets of tinfoil, then set aside.

In a large mixing bowl or the bowl of a stand mixer, put the 4 blocks of cream cheese and beat on low until they look soft and creamy, about 2 minutes. Add the sugar, coconut extract, vanilla and salt and beat on low until very creamy, 3 to 4 minutes. While still beating on low, add the eggs and yolks, one at a time, ensuring that each egg is fully incorporated before adding the next and that you are scraping down the bowl as necessary.

Add the coconut milk and sour cream, then beat on low until the cheesecake filling looks creamy, smooth and uniform. Finally, add in the cornstarch and beat on low one last time until well combined.

(continued)

WHIPPED COCONUT TOPPING

1⅓ cups (400 ml) canned coconut milk

2 tbsp (16 g) confectioners' sugar

½ cup (47 g) toasted coconut flakes

Pour the filling over top of the cooled crust in the springform pan, then place the cheesecake into a large roasting pan. Pour enough boiling water into the roasting pan so that it reaches about halfway up the outside of the springform pan. Place into the oven to bake for 1 hour and 30 minutes. When the cheesecake is done it should still be a little jiggly in the center.

When done, turn the oven off and lightly crack the oven open to allow the cheesecake to slowly cool for about an hour. After an hour, remove the cheesecake from the oven and water bath. Place onto the counter to cool to room temperature. Once at room temperature, wrap with plastic wrap and place in the fridge for at least 6 hours or preferably overnight.

WHIPPED COCONUT TOPPING

Place the can of coconut milk into the fridge overnight. The purpose of this is to make separating the solid coconut cream from the liquid easier, as well as ensuring the coconut cream is cold enough to allow proper whipping.

The next day, when you are ready to serve the cheesecake, remove the can from the fridge and poke two holes in the bottom of the can using a can punch. Drain the liquid from the can. After all of the liquid has been drained and only the solid cream remains, use a can opener to open the can, then scoop out the solid cream into a mixing bowl or stand mixer.

Add the confectioners' sugar to the coconut cream, then beat on medium until fluffy looking. Spoon the topping onto the cheesecake, top with toasted coconut flakes and serve.

NO-BAKE CHOCOLATE CHIP COOKIE DOUGH CHEESECAKE

This no-bake cheesecake is a chocolate lovers' dream. It has a crumbly chocolate cookie crust, a thick layer of chocolate chip cookie dough, a light yet rich milk chocolate cheesecake layer and finally, a generous drizzling of ganache!

MAKES 1 (9-INCH [23-CM]) CHEESECAKE

CHOCOLATE CRUST

2 cups (250 g) chocolate wafer cookie crumbs, sifted

6 tbsp (90 ml) unsalted butter, melted

COOKIE DOUGH

2 cups (440 g) packed light brown sugar

1½ cups (340 g) unsalted butter, at room temperature

3 tbsp (45 ml) heavy cream

2 tbsp (30 ml) vanilla extract

1 tsp table salt

3 cups (360 g) heat-treated all-purpose flour (see Note)

1½ cups (263 g) mini chocolate chips

CHOCOLATE CHEESECAKE

1¾ cups (300 g) milk chocolate chips

1 cup (240 ml) heavy cream, chilled

3 (8-oz [226-g]) blocks cream cheese, well softened

1 cup (120 g) confectioners' sugar

3 tbsp (45 ml) unsalted butter, melted

2 tbsp (30 ml) sour cream

2 tbsp (11 g) Dutch process cocoa powder, sifted

CHOCOLATE CRUST

In a mixing bowl, combine the cookie crumbs and melted butter, then work together with your hands or a fork until the mixture resembles wet sand. Press the crust into the bottom of a 9-inch (23-cm) springform pan, then place into the freezer for 30 minutes.

COOKIE DOUGH

In a medium mixing bowl, cream together the brown sugar, butter, cream, vanilla and salt until smooth. Add in the flour, then mix until well combined. Fold in the mini chocolate chips.

Press two-thirds of the cookie dough into the springform pan over the top of the chocolate cookie crust (reserve the rest for decorating). Place into the fridge for 1 hour.

CHOCOLATE CHEESECAKE

Add the chocolate chips to a microwave-proof bowl and place in the microwave for 1 to 2 minutes, or until melted (check at 1 minute, stir and heat for another minute, if needed). Set aside.

Pour the heavy cream into the bowl of a stand mixer or mixing bowl, then beat on medium-high until stiff peaks form. Set aside.

Add the 3 blocks of softened cream cheese and confectioners' sugar to a large mixing bowl. Using a hand mixer, beat on low until it looks smooth and creamy. Add in the melted chocolate chips, melted butter, sour cream and sifted cocoa powder, then beat on low until smooth. Fold in the whipped cream until well combined and uniform.

Pour the cheesecake batter over the top of the cookie dough layer in the springform pan, then cover the pan with plastic wrap and place into the fridge overnight to set up.

(continued)

CHOCOLATE GANACHE

4 oz (113 g) semisweet chocolate,
finely chopped

½ cup (120 ml) heavy cream

4 oz (113 g) assorted chocolate,
for decorating (optional)

CHOCOLATE GANACHE

Place the chopped chocolate into a heatproof bowl. Set aside.

In a small saucepan over medium heat, bring the heavy cream to a simmer. Remove from the heat immediately and pour into the bowl with the chocolate. Allow to sit for 2 minutes, then using a whisk, stir together until the ganache looks smooth. Allow the ganache to cool for 20 to 30 minutes before assembly.

ASSEMBLY

Remove the cheesecake from the springform pan. Place it onto a serving platter, then pour the cooled ganache over the top. Using a small cookie scoop, scoop the remaining cookie dough into balls and place them on top of the cheesecake, then add pieces of chocolate to decorate, if desired.

Note: *To heat treat flour, place it in a microwave-safe bowl and put it in the microwave. Heat the flour for 1 minute and 15 seconds, stirring it every 15 seconds. When ready, the flour should be at 160°F (71°C) for proper pasteurization for consumption without baking. Allow it to cool to room temperature before using.*

BURNT SUGAR CRÈME BRÛLÉE CHEESECAKE

What could possibly be better than cheesecake? Obviously a crème brûlée cheesecake! This richly creamy dessert is speckled with little pieces of vanilla bean, sits atop a buttery graham cracker crust and is topped with a torched caramelized sugar topping.

MAKES 1 (9-INCH [23-CM]) CHEESECAKE

GRAHAM CRACKER CRUST

1¾ cups (230 g) graham cracker crumbs

¼ cup (50 g) white sugar

½ cup (120 ml) unsalted butter, melted

VANILLA CHEESECAKE

4 (8-oz [226-g]) blocks cream cheese, well softened

1½ cups (300 g) white sugar

1 tbsp (15 ml) vanilla bean paste or extract

¼ tsp table salt

3 large eggs, at room temperature

2 large egg yolks, at room temperature

¾ cup (180 ml) heavy cream

¾ cup (180 ml) sour cream

1 tbsp (8 g) cornstarch

GRAHAM CRACKER CRUST

Preheat the oven to 350°F (175°C). In a medium bowl, combine the graham cracker crumbs and sugar and whisk until well combined. Pour the melted butter into the bowl, then mix with a fork, or your hands, until the butter is well dispersed and the mixture resembles wet sand.

Grease a 9-inch or 10-inch (23- or 25-cm) springform pan, then add the crust into the pan and press it down evenly into the bottom. Use a flat-bottomed measuring cup to really compact the crust down. Put the crust in the oven to bake for 10 minutes. Remove it from the oven and allow it to cool to room temperature.

VANILLA CHEESECAKE

Turn the oven down to 325°F (160°C). Prepare the cooled springform pan (with crust) by wrapping the bottom of the pan with two sheets of tinfoil, then set aside.

In a large mixing bowl or stand mixer, add the 4 blocks of cream cheese and beat on low until it looks soft and creamy, about 2 minutes. Add the sugar, vanilla paste and salt and beat on low until very creamy, 3 to 4 minutes. While still beating on low, add the eggs and yolks, one at a time, ensuring that each egg is fully incorporated before adding the next and that you are scraping down the bowl as necessary.

Add the heavy cream and sour cream, then beat on low until the cheesecake filling looks creamy, smooth and uniform. Finally, add in cornstarch and beat on low one last time until the cornstarch is well combined.

(continued)

CRÈME BRÛLÉE TOPPING
⅓ to ½ cup (67 to 100 g)
superfine sugar

Pour the filling over top of the cooled crust in the springform pan, then place the cheesecake into a large roasting pan. Pour enough boiling water into the roasting pan so that it reaches about halfway up the outside of the springform pan. Place it into the oven to bake for 1 hour and 30 minutes. When the cheesecake is done it should still be a little jiggly in the center.

When done, turn the oven off and lightly crack the oven open to allow the cheesecake to slowly cool for about an hour. After an hour, remove the cheesecake from the oven and water bath and place it onto the counter to cool to room temperature. Once at room temperature, wrap the pan with plastic wrap and put in the fridge for at least 6 hours or preferably overnight.

CRÈME BRÛLÉE TOPPING

At serving time, after the cheesecake is completely cooled, remove it from the springform pan. Sprinkle the top of the cheesecake with a thin layer of superfine sugar, then torch carefully with a kitchen torch until the topping is caramelized. Serve it immediately for best results.

"WAKE ME UP" NO-BAKE TIRAMISU CHEESECAKE

I like to consider myself a true tiramisu connoisseur, some may even call me a tiramisu snob. With such a title, it was of utmost importance that I made a tiramisu-inspired cheesecake that would satisfy even the harshest critics. Let me tell you, I did just that. This no-bake tiramisu cheesecake features a silky coffee-infused mascarpone filling that surrounds an espresso-drenched ladyfinger layer. It sits atop a chocolate crust, and is finished with chocolate ganache and a dreamy whipped cream.

MAKES 1 (9-INCH [23-CM]) CHEESECAKE

CHOCOLATE CRUST

2 cups (250 g) sifted chocolate wafer cookie crumbs

6 tbsp (90 ml) unsalted butter, melted

TIRAMISU CHEESECAKE FILLING

1¼ cups (300 ml) heavy cream, chilled

2 cups (460 g) mascarpone cheese, softened

1 cup (232 g) cream cheese, softened

½ cup (100 g) white sugar

2 tbsp (16 g) confectioners' sugar

¼ cup (60 ml) sour cream

1 tbsp (15 ml) Kahlúa or cold strong coffee

1 tsp vanilla extract

CHOCOLATE GANACHE

½ cup (120 ml) heavy cream

2 tbsp (28 g) unsalted butter, at room temperature

4 oz (113 g) semisweet chocolate, finely chopped

CHOCOLATE CRUST

Add the cookie crumbs and melted butter into a mixing bowl, then work together with your hands or a fork until the mixture resembles wet sand. Press the crust into the bottom of a 9-inch (23-cm) springform pan, then put in the freezer for 30 minutes.

TIRAMISU CHEESECAKE FILLING

Pour the heavy cream into the bowl of a stand mixer or mixing bowl, then beat on medium-high until stiff peaks form. Set aside.

In a large mixing bowl, combine the mascarpone, cream cheese, white sugar and confectioners' sugar. Using a hand mixer, beat on low until it looks smooth and creamy. Add in the sour cream, Kahlúa and vanilla, then beat on low until smooth. Fold in the whipped cream until well combined and uniform. Cover and place into the fridge to keep cool.

CHOCOLATE GANACHE

In a medium saucepan over medium heat, combine the cream and butter. Heat until the mixture begins to bubble.

Put the chopped chocolate in a medium mixing bowl, then pour the hot liquid over it. Stir lightly with a spatula, then let the mixture sit for 3 minutes to allow the chocolate to melt. After 3 minutes, whisk the ganache together until incorporated and smooth. Set aside to cool for 30 to 60 minutes, or until just barely warm.

(continued)

ESPRESSO-SOAKED LADYFINGERS

⅓ cup (80 ml) boiling water

2 tbsp (25 g) white sugar

1 tbsp (6 g) instant coffee powder

1 tbsp (15 ml) Kahlúa

⅔ cup (160 ml) ice-cold water

12 to 14 ladyfingers

1 tbsp (5 g) cocoa powder

WHIPPED CREAM TOPPING

1¼ cups (300 ml) heavy cream

3 tbsp (23 g) confectioners' sugar

Cocoa powder, for garnish

ESPRESSO-SOAKED LADYFINGERS AND ASSEMBLY

In a heatproof glass or bowl, mix together the boiling water, sugar, coffee powder and Kahlúa. Stir until the sugar and coffee powder completely dissolve, then add the ice-cold water. Stir to combine and transfer to an oblong-shaped dish.

Begin assembling the cheesecake by pouring half of the tiramisu cheesecake filling over the cold chocolate crust. Dip the ladyfingers into the espresso mixture and place over the top of the tiramisu cheesecake filling. Dust the cocoa powder over top, then top with the remaining tiramisu cheesecake filling. Next, pour the chocolate ganache over the top and smooth it out with a spatula. Place the cheesecake into the fridge overnight to set up.

WHIPPED CREAM TOPPING

At serving time, put the heavy cream and confectioners' sugar into a stand mixer or mixing bowl. Beat on medium-high until stiff peaks form. Spread on top of the cooled cheesecake, then dust with cocoa powder. Enjoy the cheesecake immediately or keep covered in the fridge.

NO OVEN REQUIRED:
No-Bake
DESSERTS

*Who said that baking requires actual baking?! This chapter features
a plethora of desserts that require minimal cooking and absolutely no
baking! You'll find no-bake truffles and a multitude of no-churn ice cream
recipes inspired by all those classic dessert favorites that we know and
love! Love key lime pie, but can't be bothered to make a crust or cook the
lime curd? Tangy Key Lime Pie Ice Cream (page 146) is the answer for you.
Feeling like a good ol' classic cheesecake but you don't want to spend hours
prepping and baking? New York–Style Cheesecake Ice Cream (page 145)
is here for you! Forgot to pick up your favorite peanut butter treat at the
store? My Chocolate-Covered Peanut Butter Truffles (page 150)
got you covered.*

SUMMERY FRESH STRAWBERRY-RHUBARB PIE ICE CREAM

The classic combo of rhubarb and strawberries is typically reserved for summertime pies, but this strawberry-rhubarb ice cream definitely gives pie a run for its money! This no-churn recipe features bright, fresh strawberries and wonderfully tart rhubarb, cooked down into a jammy sauce that is sweet yet balanced. This sauce is folded into the easy-to-make ice cream batter and popped into the freezer to set. The final ice cream is extraordinarily creamy, fruity and bursting with summer-time freshness!

MAKES 8 TO 10 SERVINGS

1½ cups (270 g) hulled and small diced strawberries

1½ cups (183 g) small diced rhubarb

3 tbsp (45 g) white sugar

Juice of ½ lemon

2 cups (480 ml) whipping cream

1 tsp vanilla extract

Pinch table salt

1 (14-oz [415-ml]) can sweetened condensed milk

In a medium saucepan over medium-low heat, combine the strawberries, rhubarb, sugar and lemon juice. Allow the mixture to simmer for about 15 minutes. When done, the compote should be quite cooked down and thickened. Transfer the compote to a bowl and place it in the fridge to cool down to room temperature or colder, about 1 hour.

In the bowl of a stand mixer or a large bowl, combine the whipping cream, vanilla and salt and beat until stiff peaks have formed.

Add the cooled compote and sweetened condensed milk to the whipped cream and, using a rubber spatula, fold them all together until well combined.

Pour the ice cream batter into a 9 x 5–inch (23 x 13–cm) loaf pan, cover with plastic wrap, and place into the freezer to harden for at least 6 hours, or preferably overnight.

RUM-SPIKED BANANAS FOSTER ICE CREAM

Rich caramelized bananas are mixed together with creamy dulce de leche, sweet dark rum and, of course, a rich creamy ice cream base to create a dessert that any banana lover will not be able to get enough of!

MAKES 8 TO 10 SERVINGS

BANANAS FOSTER FILLING

¼ cup (57 g) unsalted butter, at room temperature

⅓ cup (73 g) packed dark brown sugar

1 tbsp (15 ml) water

¼ tsp cinnamon

1 slightly underripe banana, sliced into ½-inch (1.3-cm) slices

⅓ cup (80 ml) rum

¼ tsp vanilla extract

¼ tsp banana extract

ICE CREAM

1¼ cups (300 ml) dulce de leche

1 large overripe banana

1 tbsp (15 ml) dark rum

½ tsp vanilla extract

¼ tsp banana extract

Pinch table salt

2 cups (480 ml) heavy cream, very chilled

BANANAS FOSTER FILLING

In a large pan over medium heat, combine the butter, brown sugar, water and cinnamon. Heat the mixture, while continuously stirring, until the brown sugar fully dissolves and is no longer grainy, 5 to 7 minutes.

Add the sliced banana to the pan and toss to coat it in the sugar syrup. Continue cooking, while gently moving the bananas around, until they soften and begin to brown.

Remove the pan from the heat source, then add the rum to the pan. Using a long-stemmed lighter, carefully ignite the rum. Carefully return the pan back to the heat, and gently shake the pan until the flames dissipate.

Continue heating, while stirring or shaking, for an additional 3 minutes, then remove from the heat and add in the vanilla and banana extract.

Transfer the bananas Foster into a bowl and place it into the fridge for 3 to 4 hours.

ICE CREAM

In a blender, combine the dulce de leche, banana, rum, vanilla, banana extract and salt. Blend until smooth.

Meanwhile, pour the chilled heavy cream into a large bowl or the bowl of a stand mixer and beat on medium speed until stiff peaks have formed.

Pour the dulce de leche mixture and the cooled bananas Foster into the whipped cream, then fold together with a spatula until fully combined.

Pour the ice cream batter into a 9 x 5–inch (23 x 13–cm) loaf pan. Cover the pan with plastic and place into the freezer to set for at least 8 hours, or preferably overnight.

NEW YORK–STYLE CHEESECAKE ICE CREAM

Where are my fellow cheesecake connoisseurs at? Now, don't get me wrong, I love classic baked cheesecake, but sometimes I just can't be bothered to make one. Enter: New York–Style Cheesecake Ice Cream. This no-churn style ice cream has all those classic rich cheesecake flavors, but with half of the effort and absolutely no cooking involved!

MAKES 8 TO 10 SERVINGS

1 (14-oz [415-ml]) can sweetened condensed milk

1½ cups (350 g) cream cheese, softened

Pinch table salt

1½ cups (360 ml) heavy cream, very chilled

6 tbsp (50 g) graham cracker crumbs

2 tsp (8 g) white sugar

2 tbsp (30 ml) unsalted butter, melted

In a medium-large mixing bowl, combine the sweetened condensed milk, softened cream cheese and salt. Whisk them together to combine until very smooth.

Meanwhile, into a large bowl or the bowl of a stand mixer, pour the chilled heavy cream and beat on medium speed until stiff peaks have formed.

Pour the sweetened condensed milk mixture into the whipped cream, then fold together with a spatula until fully combined. Set aside.

In a medium mixing bowl, whisk together the graham cracker crumbs and sugar. Pour the melted butter over the top and work it into the mixture with your hands or a fork.

Pour half of the ice cream batter into a 9 x 5–inch (23 x 13–cm) loaf pan. Top it with half of the graham cracker crumble. Pour the remaining ice cream batter on top, then finish with the remaining graham cracker crumble.

Cover the pan with plastic, and place it into the freezer to set for at least 8 hours, or preferably overnight!

TANGY KEY LIME PIE ICE CREAM

This velvety ice cream features a delicious tangy citrus flavor that is perfectly balanced by the richness of the condensed milk and heavy cream. This Key lime pie–inspired treat is full of sweet, tart lime flavor, which pairs wonderfully with the rich creamy ice cream base. If you cannot find Key limes, feel free to substitute with regular (Persian) limes.

MAKES 8 TO 10 SERVINGS

1 (14-oz [415-ml]) can sweetened condensed milk

½ cup (120 ml) sour cream

Zest of 13 Key limes, about ¼ cup (60 ml)

Juice of 13 Key limes, about ½ cup (120 ml)

Pinch table salt

Green food coloring (optional)

1½ cups (360 ml) heavy cream, very chilled

6 tbsp (50 g) graham cracker crumbs

2 tsp (8 g) white sugar

2 tbsp (30 ml) unsalted butter, melted

In a medium-large mixing bowl, combine the sweetened condensed milk, sour cream, lime zest, lime juice, salt and food coloring, if using. Whisk them together to combine.

Meanwhile, into a large bowl or the bowl of a stand mixer, pour the chilled heavy cream and beat on medium speed until stiff peaks have formed.

Pour the sweetened condensed milk mixture into the whipped cream, then fold together with a spatula until fully combined. Set aside.

In a medium mixing bowl, whisk together the graham cracker crumbs and sugar. Pour the melted butter over the top and work it into the mixture with your hands or a fork.

Pour half of the ice cream batter into a 9 x 5–inch (23 x 13–cm) loaf pan. Top with half of the graham cracker crumble. Pour the remaining ice cream batter on top, then finish with the remaining graham cracker crumble.

Cover the pan with plastic and place it into the freezer to set for at least 8 hours, or preferably overnight.

NUTTY PECAN PIE SUNDAE

Craving pecan pie, but can't be bothered with all the pesky prep and baking?
I've got you covered. This sundae is jam-packed with warm, creamy caramel,
crunchy toasted pecans and silky vanilla ice cream!

MAKES 4 SUNDAES

SALTED CARAMEL

1 cup (200 g) white sugar

¼ cup (60 ml) water

6 tbsp (85 g) unsalted butter, at room temperature and cubed

½ cup (120 ml) heavy cream

1 tsp vanilla extract

½ tsp table salt

PECAN PIE SUNDAE

1 cup (115 g) roughly chopped pecans

2 tbsp (28 g) unsalted butter, at room temperature

¼ tsp cinnamon

Pinch table salt

8 to 12 scoops of vanilla ice cream

SALTED CARAMEL

In a large saucepan over medium heat, combine the sugar and water. Stir occasionally until the sugar has dissolved and the mixture begins to boil.

Once the mixture begins to boil, turn the heat up to medium-high and allow the mixture to continue to boil, taking care not to stir it, until it turns amber in color. (Stirring the mixture will cause crystallization, so refrain from stirring.)

Once the mixture has become amber in color (at a temperature of 360°F [182°C] on a candy thermometer), add the cubed butter and mix very vigorously to combine. (Be careful, however, because the mixture will bubble and rise up rapidly when you add the butter.) If the butter seems to be separating from the caramel, remove it from the heat, then whisk vigorously until it comes together.

Next, slowly drizzle in the heavy cream while whisking (it will bubble rapidly again). Then add the vanilla and salt. Whisk the caramel mixture until smooth and well combined. Remove the caramel from the heat, then set aside while you toast the pecans.

PECAN PIE SUNDAE

In a medium pan over medium heat, combine the pecans, butter, cinnamon and salt. Heat while continuously stirring and tossing until the pecans begin to brown and become very fragrant.

Pour a third of the salted caramel into the toasted pecans, then stir to combine.

Put two or three scoops of ice cream per serving into a bowl or sundae glass, then top with a quarter of pecan mixture and a quarter of the remaining warm salted caramel.

Note: Salted caramel can be stored in the fridge for 2 weeks and reheated in the microwave when needed.

CHOCOLATE-COVERED PEANUT BUTTER TRUFFLES

Say goodbye to store-bought peanut butter chocolate treats, because these
peanut butter truffles will Blow. Your. Mind. Each little truffle is made from almond flour,
peanut butter and sugar and then covered in a thin coating of velvety chocolate,
making for an easy, no-bake treat!

MAKES 20 TRUFFLES

PEANUT BUTTER TRUFFLES

1⅓ cups (160 g) confectioners' sugar

1¼ cups (322 g) smooth peanut butter

⅔ cup (63 g) almond flour

1 tsp vanilla extract

¼ tsp table salt

CHOCOLATE COATING

14 oz (400 g) semisweet chocolate, finely chopped

1 tbsp (14 g) coconut oil

Crushed peanuts, for garnish

PEANUT BUTTER TRUFFLES

In a medium mixing bowl, beat together the sugar, peanut butter, almond flour, vanilla and salt until smooth and well combined.

Using a ¾-ounce (22-ml) cookie scoop, scoop out 20 scoops of peanut butter dough. Roll each scoop into a ball with your hands, then place onto a parchment-lined baking sheet. Place the peanut butter truffle–filled baking sheet into the freezer for 2 to 4 hours.

CHOCOLATE COATING

Add the chopped chocolate and coconut oil into a heatproof bowl. Set the bowl over the top of a simmering pot of water, making sure a tight seal forms and that the bottom of the stand mixer bowl is not actually touching the water.

Heat the chocolate, while stirring, until it is fully melted and is incorporated with the coconut oil. Remove from the heat.

While working quickly, use a candy-making utensil or a fork to dip each semi-frozen truffle into the chocolate, then place it back onto the parchment to set. After all of the truffles have been dipped, drizzle the remaining chocolate over the truffles with a spoon, then immediately top them with crushed peanuts.

For the best texture, keep the truffles in a lidded container in the fridge.

DECADENT COOKIE DOUGH TRUFFLES

In my opinion, the best part about making cookies is eating the cookie dough! These chocolate-covered cookie dough truffles are the perfect little treat for my fellow cookie dough lovers who can't help but always sneak dough out of the bowl. This recipe is made without eggs and uses heat-treated flour for safe consumption.

MAKES 28 TRUFFLES

COOKIE DOUGH

1½ cups (330 g) packed light brown sugar

1 cup (227 g) unsalted butter, at room temperature

¼ cup (60 ml) heavy cream

1 tbsp (15 ml) vanilla extract

¾ tsp table salt

2 cups (240 g) heat treated all-purpose flour (see Note)

½ cup (88 g) mini chocolate chips

CHOCOLATE COATING

14 oz (400 g) semisweet chocolate, finely chopped

1 tbsp (14 g) coconut oil

Flaky sea salt, for garnish

COOKIE DOUGH

In a medium mixing bowl, cream together the brown sugar, butter, cream, vanilla and salt until smooth. Add in the flour, then mix until well combined. Fold in the chocolate chips.

Using a ¾-ounce (22-ml) cookie scoop, scoop out 28 scoops of cookie dough. Roll each scoop into a ball with your hands, then place it onto a parchment-lined baking sheet. Place the cookie dough-filled baking sheet into the freezer for 30 minutes to an hour.

CHOCOLATE COATING

In a heat-proof bowl, combine the chopped chocolate and coconut oil. Set the bowl over the top of a simmering pot of water, making sure a tight seal forms and that the bottom of the stand mixer bowl is not actually touching the water.

Heat the chocolate, while stirring, until it is fully melted and incorporated with the coconut oil. Remove it from the heat.

Using candy-making utensils or a fork, dip each semi-frozen truffle into the chocolate, then place it back onto the parchment to set. After all of the truffles have been dipped, drizzle the remaining chocolate over the truffles with a spoon, then immediately top with flaky sea salt.

For the best texture, keep the truffles in a lidded container in the fridge.

Note: To heat treat flour, place the flour in a microwave-safe bowl and place it in the microwave. Heat the flour in the microwave for 1 minute and 15 seconds, stirring every 15 seconds. When ready, the flour should be at 160°F (71°C) for proper pasteurization for consumption. Allow the flour to cool to room temperature before using.

Tempting
TARTS & SCONES

When I named this chapter I was not exaggerating about the "tempting" part! What could be more tempting than a luscious, buttery scone that seemingly has a million little flaky layers and is speckled with melty pieces of chocolate (page 168)? Or an ultra-rich chocolate and espresso ganache that is encased by a melt-in-your-mouth tender chocolate crust and further topped with an extremely generous helping of mascarpone whipped cream (page 159)? This chapter features tarts and scones that are rich in flavor, full of butter and, of course, tempting AF!

VELVETY SMOOTH CRÈME BRÛLÉE TART

This tart is like the delicious love child of crème brûlée and pie! This recipe features an ultra-buttery shortbread crust that is a breeze to make and shape. The silky smooth crème brûlée filling has a rich, creamy flavor and is filled with just the right amount of vanilla to make your mouth water. And, of course, it's not crème brûlée without that delicately crisp caramelized sugar topping! This recipe features a torchless method to create that perfect golden, glassy top. Make sure you serve this dessert immediately after topping it as the caramelized sugar loses its crispness quickly.

MAKES 1 (9-INCH [23-CM]) TART

SHORTBREAD CRUST
1 cup plus 2 tbsp (140 g) all-purpose flour

Pinch table salt

⅓ cup (66 g) white sugar

½ cup (114 g) unsalted butter, at room temperature

½ tsp vanilla extract

1 large egg white

CRÈME BRÛLÉE TART FILLING
4 large egg yolks

¼ cup (50 g) white sugar

1⅓ cups (320 ml) heavy cream

1 tsp vanilla bean paste

Pinch table salt

SHORTBREAD CRUST

Preheat the oven to 350°F (175°C). Add flour and salt to a bowl and whisk to combine. In a separate bowl, cream together the sugar, butter and vanilla until just combined. Add the dry ingredients and beat to combine until a crumbly dough forms.

Place the dough into a 9-inch (23-cm) tart pan and spread it evenly with your hands across the entire bottom and up the sides. Place the tart pan onto a baking sheet and then place into the oven for 13 minutes. Remove from the oven, and then while the crust is still warm, press down any puffed-up parts using a flat-bottomed glass or measuring cup. Lightly brush with egg white, then allow to cool completely before adding the tart filling, about 45 minutes.

CRÈME BRÛLÉE TART FILLING

Turn the oven down to 275°F (135°C). In a mixing bowl, whisk together the egg yolks and sugar until smooth. Next, add the cream, vanilla paste and salt, then whisk again until smooth.

Pour the filling through a fine-mesh sieve into the cooled crust, lightly using your fingers to pop any bubbles on the surface, then return the tart to the oven to bake for 40 to 45 minutes. When done, the tart should still be slightly jiggly in the center.

Remove the tart from the oven and allow it to come to room temperature on the counter, about 1½ hours. When the tart reaches room temperature, wrap the top with plastic wrap, then place into the fridge to cool for at least 6 hours, preferably overnight, or up to 2 days.

(continued)

VELVETY SMOOTH CRÈME BRÛLÉE TART (CONTINUED)

CARAMELIZED SUGAR TOPPING

6 tbsp (85 g) white sugar
1 tbsp (15 ml) water
1 tsp light corn syrup

CARAMELIZED SUGAR TOPPING

At serving time, put all the caramelized sugar topping ingredients into a small saucepan over medium heat. Whisk to combine, then allow the mixture to come to a boil. Without stirring, allow the sugar syrup to caramelize into a deep amber color.

Remove the tart from the fridge and remove the plastic wrap. Immediately pour the hot caramelized sugar over the tart and begin to angle and rotate the pan until the sugar topping is evenly spread onto the entire filling. Allow the sugar topping to harden completely, about 1 minute, then serve immediately.

ESPRESSO-DRENCHED TIRAMISU TART

My number-one favorite dessert is tiramisu. The aromatic flavors of coffee mixed with rich chocolate and silky whipped cream or custard are truly what I would call a dream come true. This tart has a tender chocolate crust that is filled with espresso-infused chocolate ganache. The best part? A sky-high piling of mascarpone whipped cream!

MAKES 1 (9-INCH [23-CM]) TART

CHOCOLATE CRUST

1¾ cups (210 g) all-purpose flour

¾ cup (90 g) confectioners' sugar

⅓ cup (25 g) cocoa powder, preferably Dutch process, sifted

¼ tsp table salt

½ cup (114 g) cold unsalted butter, cubed

1 large egg

CHOCOLATE CRUST

In a mixing bowl, whisk together the flour, confectioners' sugar, cocoa powder and salt until well combined. Add the butter and work it into the flour mixture using your fingers, until it all resembles sand. Add the egg, then work the egg into the mixture with your hands until it is well dispersed and the dough comes together. Knead the dough a few times until it looks smooth.

Remove the dough from the bowl, then form it into a disk shape with your hands. Wrap the disk in plastic wrap and place into the fridge for 2 hours.

Remove and unwrap the dough. Place the dough in between two silicone mats and allow it to warm up on the counter for 5 minutes. Roll the dough out between the silicone mats to be about a 12-inch (30-cm)-wide circle. Remove the top silicone mat, then transfer the dough into a 9-inch (23-cm) tart pan by flipping the silicone mat with the dough over into the tart pan and then peeling off the silicone mat. Carefully shape the dough into the pan and press against the bottom and sides of the tart pan. Remove the excess dough using a knife. If the dough tore at all during the transfer, patch the holes with the excess dough you cut off. Prick the dough a few times with a fork.

Preheat the oven to 350°F (175°C). Place the dough into the freezer for 15 minutes.

Remove the crust from the freezer, place a piece of parchment in it, place pie weights (or dried beans) over the parchment and then bake for 25 minutes. Allow the crust to cool completely before adding the filling, about 2 hours.

(continued)

CHOCOLATE-ESPRESSO FILLING

12 oz (340 g) semisweet chocolate, finely chopped

¾ cup (180 ml) heavy cream

¼ cup (60 ml) Kahlúa

¼ cup (57 g) unsalted butter, at room temperature

2 tbsp (30 g) white sugar

2 tsp (4 g) instant coffee powder

Pinch table salt

MASCARPONE WHIPPED CREAM

1 cup (240 ml) heavy cream, chilled

½ cup (60 g) confectioners' sugar

1 cup (232 g) mascarpone cheese, slightly softened

1 tsp vanilla extract

Shaved dark chocolate, for garnish (optional)

Chocolate sauce, for garnish (optional)

CHOCOLATE-ESPRESSO FILLING

Put the chopped chocolate into a heatproof bowl and set aside.

In a medium saucepan over medium heat, combine the cream, Kahlúa, butter, sugar, coffee powder and salt. Bring to a simmer, then remove from the heat and pour over the chopped chocolate. Stir the mixture lightly with a rubber spatula, then allow it to sit for 3 minutes to allow the chocolate to melt. After 3 minutes, whisk the ganache until it comes together and is smooth.

Pour the warm ganache over the cooled chocolate crust, cover lightly with plastic wrap and place into the fridge for at least 6 hours, or preferably overnight.

MASCARPONE WHIPPED CREAM

Into the bowl of a stand mixer or a mixing bowl, pour the cream and add the confectioners' sugar, then beat on medium-high until stiff peaks form. Add in the mascarpone cheese and vanilla, then beat until well combined, about 2 more minutes.

Dollop the mascarpone whipped cream onto the cooled tart, then garnish with shaved chocolate and chocolate sauce if desired.

IT'S MY BIRTHDAY CAKE SCONES

Sweet, speckled with rainbow sprinkles and full of tender flaky layers—these scones will put a smile on anyone's face! These scones get their birthday cake flavor thanks to the large addition of vanilla extract. The icing on the birthday cake, as they say, comes from the generous helping of rainbow sprinkles, both in the scones and on top.

MAKES 8 SCONES

BIRTHDAY CAKE SCONES

1½ cups (180 g) all-purpose flour, plus more for dusting

1 cup (120 g) pastry flour

½ cup (100 g) white sugar

1 tbsp (14 g) baking powder

¼ tsp table salt

½ cup (114 g) cold unsalted butter, cubed

6 tbsp (72 g) rainbow sprinkles

1 tbsp (15 ml) vanilla extract

¾ cup (180 ml) cold heavy cream, plus more if needed

VANILLA GLAZE

1½ cups (180 g) confectioners' sugar, sifted

7 to 8 tsp (35 to 40 ml) hot water

½ tsp vanilla extract

Rainbow sprinkles

BIRTHDAY CAKE SCONES

Prepare a large baking sheet with parchment paper. Meanwhile, in a large mixing bowl, combine the all-purpose and pastry flours, sugar, baking powder and salt and whisk well to combine. Add in the cold butter cubes and work the butter into the flour with your hands or a pastry cutter. Work the butter until it is crumbly and about the size of peas. Add in the sprinkles and toss until they are well dispersed throughout.

In a small bowl, stir together the vanilla and the heavy cream. Slowly drizzle the vanilla-cream into the flour mixture while tossing it with a fork until a shaggy dough comes together. If the dough does not want to come together, add more cream, about 1 teaspoon at a time, (it should still be shaggy and slightly dry looking, however).

When the dough comes together, turn it out onto a well-floured work surface. Pat the dough to form a smooth 6- to 7-inch (15- to 18-cm) disk, that is about 1 inch (2.5 cm) thick (make sure every once in a while that the dough isn't sticking to your work surface). Using a bench scraper or a knife, cut the dough into 8 equal pieces. Then, transfer the wedges, spaced apart, onto the prepared baking sheet and place into the freezer for 20 minutes.

Preheat the oven to 425°F (220°C).

After 20 minutes, remove the scones from the freezer and place them into the preheated oven and immediately turn the oven down to 375°F (190°C), and bake for 15 to 20 minutes, or until the edges just begin to turn slightly golden. Transfer the scones to a cooling rack and allow them to cool completely before glazing.

VANILLA GLAZE

Add the confectioners' sugar, hot water and vanilla to a medium-sized mixing bowl and whisk to combine into a thick but still fluid glaze. Pour the glaze over the cooled scones and spread the glaze out with a spoon or spatula. Top the glazed scones with more sprinkles to finish.

FLAKY APPLE PIE SCONES

These scones can be described as buttery, flaky and full of apple pie flavor thanks
to the addition of cinnamon, nutmeg and, of course, apples!

MAKES 8 SCONES

APPLE PIE SCONES

2½ cups (300 g) all-purpose flour,
plus more for dusting

½ cup (100 g) white sugar

1 tbsp (14 g) baking powder

½ tsp table salt

1 tbsp (8 g) cinnamon

¼ tsp nutmeg

7 tbsp (100 g) very cold unsalted
butter, cubed

1 cup (120 g) peeled and diced
apple, sweet-tart variety
(see Note)

1 tsp vanilla extract

¾ cup (180 ml) heavy cream,
plus more if needed

VANILLA BEAN GLAZE

1 cup (120 g) confectioners'
sugar

¼ cup (60 ml) heavy cream

½ tsp vanilla bean paste

*Note: These apple pie scones
are best when you use a sweet-
tart variety of apple that can hold
its shape during baking. Look for
varieties such as Pink Lady (my
personal choice), Braeburn or
even Honeycrisp (which is a touch
more sweet).*

APPLE PIE SCONES

Prepare a large baking sheet with parchment paper. Meanwhile, in a large
mixing bowl, combine the flour, sugar, baking powder, salt, cinnamon and
nutmeg, whisking well. Add in the cold butter cubes and work the butter into
the flour with your hands or a pastry cutter. Work the butter until it is crumbly
and about the size of peas. Add in the apple pieces and toss.

In a small bowl combine the vanilla with the heavy cream. Slowly drizzle
the vanilla-cream into the flour mixture while tossing with a fork. Press
the mixture together and knead with your hands until a shaggy dough
forms. If the dough does not want to come together, add more cream
in, about 1 teaspoon at a time, until it does (it should still be shaggy
and slightly dry looking, however).

When the dough comes together, turn it out onto a floured work surface.
Press and pat the dough to form a smooth 6- to 7-inch (15- to 18-cm)
disk that is about 1 inch (2.5 cm) thick. (Make sure every once in a while
that the dough isn't sticking to your work surface.) Using a bench
scraper or a knife, cut the dough into eight equal pieces. Then transfer
the wedges, spaced apart, onto the prepared baking sheet, and place
into the freezer for 20 minutes.

Preheat the oven to 400°F (200°C).

After 20 minutes, remove the scones from the freezer and place into the
preheated oven and bake for about 20 minutes, or until they just begin
to turn golden. Transfer the scones to a cooling rack and allow them to
cool completely before glazing.

VANILLA BEAN GLAZE

Add the confectioners' sugar, heavy cream and vanilla paste to a
medium-sized mixing bowl and whisk to combine into a thick-but-still-
fluid glaze. Pour the glaze over the cooled scones and spread the
glaze out with a spoon or spatula. Allow it to set before enjoying.

BUTTERY BANANA BREAD SCONES

This is banana bread but in scone form—truly a dessert of your dreams!
These scones are rich in classic, cozy banana bread flavor and are an absolute textural
pleasure with their flaky, buttery layers. Finished with a sweet buttered maple glaze,
these scones have a definite wow factor.

MAKES 8 SCONES

BANANA BREAD SCONES

2½ cups (300 g) all-purpose flour, plus more for dusting

½ cup (110 g) packed brown sugar

2 tsp (9 g) baking powder

½ tsp table salt

½ tsp cinnamon

7 tbsp (100 g) very cold unsalted butter, cubed

⅔ cup (160 ml) puréed very ripe banana (about 1 large banana)

⅓ cup (80 ml) heavy cream, plus more if needed

1 tsp vanilla extract

MAPLE GLAZE

2 tbsp (28 g) unsalted butter, at room temperature

2 tbsp (30 ml) maple syrup

1 cup (120 g) confectioners' sugar

1 tbsp (15 ml) heavy cream

¼ tsp maple extract

¼ cup (27 g) chopped pecans or walnuts, for garnish

BANANA BREAD SCONES

Prepare a large baking sheet with parchment paper. Meanwhile, in a large mixing bowl, add the flour, brown sugar, baking powder, salt and cinnamon and whisk well to combine. Add in the cold butter cubes, and work the butter into the flour with your hands or a pastry cutter. Work the butter until it is crumbly and about the size of peas.

In a bowl, combine the puréed banana, heavy cream and vanilla and stir well. Slowly drizzle the wet ingredients into the flour mixture, while tossing with a fork. Press together and knead with your hands until a shaggy dough comes together. If the dough does not want to come together, add more cream, about 1 teaspoon at a time, until it does (it should still be shaggy and slightly dry looking, however).

When the dough comes together, turn it out onto a floured work surface. Press and pat the dough to form a smooth 6- to 7-inch (15- to 18-cm) disk that is about 1 inch (2.5 cm) thick (make sure every once in a while that the dough isn't sticking to the work surface). Using a bench scraper or a knife, cut the dough into eight equal pieces. Then, transfer the wedges, spaced apart, onto the prepared baking sheet, and place into the freezer for 20 minutes.

Preheat the oven to 400°F (200°C).

After 20 minutes, remove the scones from the freezer and place them into the preheated oven and bake for about 20 minutes, or until they just begin to turn golden. Transfer the scones to a cooling rack and allow them to cool completely before glazing.

MAPLE GLAZE

Put the butter and maple syrup in a small saucepan over medium heat. Heat until the butter has completely melted, then take it off the heat and add in the confectioners' sugar, cream and maple extract. Whisk until smooth.

Spoon the glaze over the scones, then garnish with chopped nuts.

CHOCOLATE CHIP COOKIE SCONES

Filled to the edge with buttery, flaky layers and speckled with rich chocolate chips throughout, these cookie-inspired scones can be enjoyed as an indulgent breakfast or as an on-the-go handheld treat!

MAKES 8 SCONES

2½ cups (300 g) all-purpose flour, plus more for dusting

½ cup (100 g) white sugar

2 tsp (9 g) baking powder

½ tsp table salt

7 tbsp (100 g) very cold unsalted butter, cubed

1¼ cups (210 g) chocolate chips

1½ tsp (7.5 ml) vanilla extract

1 cup (240 ml) heavy cream, plus more if needed

2 tbsp (25 g) sanding sugar, for garnish

Prepare a large baking sheet with parchment paper. Meanwhile, in a large mixing bowl, whisk together the flour, sugar, baking powder and salt. Add in the cold butter cubes, and work the butter into the flour with your hands or a pastry cutter. Work the butter until it is crumbly and about the size of peas. Add in the chocolate chips and toss.

In a bowl, stir together the vanilla with the heavy cream. Slowly drizzle the vanilla-cream mixture into the flour mixture while tossing with a fork. Press the mixture together and knead with your hands until a shaggy dough comes together. If the dough does not want to come together, add more cream, about 1 teaspoon at a time, until it does (it should still be shaggy and slightly dry looking, however).

When the dough finally comes together, turn it out onto a floured work surface. Press and pat the dough to form a smooth 6- to 7-inch (15- to 18-cm) disk that is about 1 inch (2.5 cm) thick (make sure every once in a while that the dough isn't sticking to your work surface). Using a bench scraper or a knife, cut the dough into eight equal pieces. Then, transfer the wedges, spaced apart, onto the prepared baking sheet, and place it into the freezer for 20 minutes.

Preheat the oven to 400°F (200°C).

After 20 minutes, remove the scones from the freezer, brush with more heavy cream, sprinkle with sanding sugar and then place them into the preheated oven and bake for 18 to 20 minutes, or until they begin to turn slightly golden. Transfer the scones to a cooling rack or enjoy warm.

A Gluten-Devotee's
GUIDE TO BREAD & ROLLS

Imagine this: It's Sunday morning, your house is filled with the sweet, yeasty smell of fresh cinnamon rolls baking up in your oven. Except these aren't regular cinnamon rolls. No, they're red velvet cinnamon rolls that are a gorgeous shade of crimson and slightly infused with cocoa powder for that classic red velvet flavor (page 181). Find this recipe, along with several other gluten-filled and oh-so-sweet breads and rolls in this chapter!

SOFT AND FLUFFY PUMPKIN PIE BABKA

You simply can't go wrong with pie-flavored bread. This babka features a tender, sweet dough stuffed with a perfectly spiced pumpkin pie filling, then cut, braided and baked to create a yeasty sweet bread that is swirled throughout with goodness!

MAKES 1 (9 X 5-INCH [23 X 13-CM]) LOAF

BABKA BREAD

1 cup (240 ml) whole milk, warmed slightly

⅓ cup (80 ml) unsalted butter, melted

¼ cup (50 g) white sugar

1 large egg

2¼ tsp (9 g) instant yeast

½ tsp vanilla extract

3¼ cups (390 g) all-purpose flour, plus more for dusting

½ tsp table salt

PUMPKIN PIE FILLING

¾ cup (165 g) packed dark brown sugar

2 tsp (5 g) cinnamon

1 tsp allspice

1 tsp ground ginger

6 tbsp (91 g) pumpkin purée

In the bowl of a stand mixer, combine the milk, butter, sugar, egg, yeast and vanilla and whisk together by hand.

In a mixing bowl, whisk together the flour and salt. Add this to the stand mixer bowl, then using a large wooden spoon, mix together until a shaggy dough forms. Fit the stand mixer with the dough hook, then turn it on to medium. Beat the dough for 8 to 10 minutes, or until the dough is smooth, elastic and slightly tacky. Transfer the dough to a large greased bowl, cover with plastic wrap, then place in a warm area to rise for 1 to 2 hours, or until the dough is doubled in size.

In a medium mixing bowl, whisk together the brown sugar, cinnamon, allspice and ginger until well combined. Set aside.

Prepare a 9 x 5–inch (23 x 13–cm) loaf pan with grease and parchment paper. Turn the dough out onto a lightly floured work surface, and roll the dough out into a 15 x 15–inch (38 x 38–cm) square.

Spread the pumpkin purée over the dough, leaving a 1-inch (2.5-cm) strip along the top. Sprinkle the spiced brown sugar over the pumpkin purée. Brush the bare 1-inch (2.5-cm) strip with a bit of water. Roll the dough away from you into a log (try to maintain even thickness throughout). Pinch to seal. Using a serrated knife, slice the log in half lengthwise. Place the sliced halves faceup and side by side. Form an X with the two strips. Working from the center out, interweave the two strips by folding them over one another, alternating back and forth. When at the end, pinch the ends together. Repeat on the other half.

Transfer the braided dough into the prepared loaf pan, cover lightly with plastic wrap and place into a warm place to rise for another hour, or until nearly doubled in size. Preheat the oven to 350°F (175°C).

(continued)

SOFT AND FLUFFY PUMPKIN PIE BABKA (CONTINUED)

STREUSEL TOPPING

2 tbsp (25 g) white sugar

¼ cup (30 g) all-purpose flour

¼ tsp cinnamon

Pinch table salt

2 tbsp (28 g) cold unsalted butter, cubed

1 large egg

2 tsp (10 ml) water, for egg wash

In a bowl, whisk together the sugar, flour, cinnamon and salt until well combined. Cut in the butter cubes using a pastry cutter, until the streusel resembles small peas. Keep cold until the bread is fully risen.

Whisk together the egg and water until foamy. Brush the proofed dough lightly with the egg wash, then sprinkle the streusel over top. Place the bread into the oven to bake for 40 to 45 minutes. Allow the babka to cool completely before slicing.

Roll the filled dough into a log

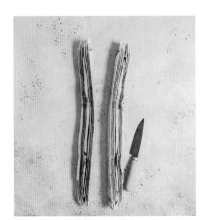

Slice the dough-log in half lengthwise

With the cut sides up, form an X

Working from the center, weave the two (bottom) halves together

Weave the remaining (top) halves together and pinch the ends

SPRINKLES GALORE BIRTHDAY CAKE ROLLS

What could be better than a rich, buttery and tender dough rolled around a birthday cake filling? This recipe uses boxed cake mix, butter and sprinkles as the filling—giving that truly authentic birthday cake flavor!

MAKES 12 ROLLS

BIRTHDAY CAKE ROLLS DOUGH

⅔ cup (160 ml) whole milk, warmed

2¼ tsp (7 g) instant yeast

¼ cup (50 g) white sugar

1 large egg

1 large egg yolk

¼ cup (60 ml) unsalted butter, melted

1 tsp vanilla extract

3 cups (360 g) all-purpose flour, plus more for dusting

¾ tsp table salt

¼ cup (60 ml) heavy cream (for baking)

BIRTHDAY CAKE FILLING

¾ cup (113 g) yellow cake mix

½ cup (96 g) sprinkles

6 tbsp (85 g) unsalted butter, softened

MAKING THE DOUGH

In the bowl of a stand mixer fitted with the dough hook, combine the milk, yeast, sugar, egg, egg yolk, melted butter and vanilla. Whisk together by hand to combine.

In a small mixing bowl, whisk together the flour and salt. Add to the stand mixer bowl, then using a large wooden spoon, mix together until a shaggy dough forms. Turn the stand mixer onto medium speed. Beat the dough for about 8 minutes, or until the dough is smooth, elastic and tacky.

Transfer the dough to a large greased bowl, cover with plastic wrap, then place in a warm area to rise for 1 to 2 hours, or until the dough has doubled in size.

FILLING, ROLLING AND CUTTING THE BIRTHDAY CAKE ROLLS

In a small mixing bowl, whisk together the cake mix and sprinkles. Set aside.

Prepare a 9 x 13–inch (23 x 33–cm) pan with cooking spray and parchment. Punch down the risen dough, then turn it out onto a lightly floured work surface and roll the dough into a 16 x 12–inch (40 x 30–cm) rectangle with the long side facing you.

Spread the softened butter over top of the dough, leaving about a ½-inch (1.3-cm) strip along the top, then sprinkle the cake mix/sprinkle mixture over the top of the butter and press down into the butter with your hands. Brush the bare ½-inch (1.3-cm) strip with a bit of water. Roll the dough away from you into a log (try to maintain even thickness throughout). Pinch to seal.

Using a serrated knife or string, slice the log into 12 equal-sized pieces. Place the rolls cut side up into the prepared pan, then cover lightly with plastic wrap and place into a warm spot to rise for 30 to 45 minutes, or until nearly doubled in size. Preheat the oven to 350°F (175°C).

(continued)

VANILLA FROSTING

1¼ cups (150 g) confectioners' sugar

½ cup (114 g) unsalted butter, at room temperature

2 tbsp (30 ml) heavy cream

1 tsp vanilla extract

Sprinkles, for decorating

VANILLA FROSTING

While the rolls rise and the oven preheats, make the vanilla frosting. In a medium mixing bowl, combine the confectioners' sugar, butter, cream and vanilla and beat together using a hand mixer until smooth. Cover and set aside.

BAKING THE BIRTHDAY CAKE ROLLS

Carefully remove the plastic covering the rolls and pour the heavy cream over them, then place the rolls into the oven to bake for about 25 minutes (to an internal temperature of 200°F [95°C] on a kitchen thermometer). Top the buns with the vanilla frosting while they're still warm, then decorate with the sprinkles.

PILLOWY PUMPKIN PIE CINNAMON ROLLS

If you were to ask me for a list of my favorite foods to eat, the answer would definitely include both pumpkin pie and cinnamon rolls. So, what could possibly be better than a pumpkin pie cinnamon roll?! These deliciously tender rolls feature a yeast dough that is infused with both pumpkin spice and pumpkin purée, a warmly spiced filling and, of course, a generous slathering of classic cream cheese frosting. Serve these hot for the best ooey-gooey cinnamon roll experience.

MAKES 12 ROLLS

PUMPKIN DOUGH

½ cup (120 ml) whole milk, warmed

½ cup (123 g) pumpkin purée

2¼ tsp (7 g) instant yeast

¼ cup (55 g) packed brown sugar

1 large egg

1 large egg yolk

¼ cup (60 ml) unsalted butter, melted

3¼ cups (390 g) all-purpose flour, plus more for dusting

1½ tsp (4 g) cinnamon

1 tsp allspice

½ tsp table salt

SPICED FILLING

¾ cup (165 g) packed dark brown sugar

2 tbsp (16 g) cinnamon

¼ tsp ground cloves

¼ tsp nutmeg

6 tbsp (85 g) unsalted butter, softened

MAKING THE PUMPKIN DOUGH

In the bowl of a stand mixer, whisk together by hand the milk, pumpkin purée, yeast, brown sugar, egg, egg yolk and melted butter.

In a small mixing bowl, whisk together the flour, cinnamon, allspice and salt. Add to the stand mixer bowl, then using a large wooden spoon, mix together until a shaggy dough forms. Fit the stand mixer with the dough hook and turn it on to medium. Beat the dough for about 15 minutes, or until the dough is smooth, elastic and tacky.

Transfer the dough to a large greased bowl, cover with plastic wrap and place in a warm area to rise for 1 to 2 hours, or until the dough has doubled in size.

FILLING, ROLLING AND CUTTING THE PUMPKIN ROLLS

In a small mixing bowl, whisk together the brown sugar, cinnamon, cloves and nutmeg. Set aside.

Prepare a 9 x 13–inch (23 x 33–cm) pan with cooking spray and parchment. Punch down the risen dough, then turn it out onto a lightly floured work surface and roll the dough into a 16 x 12–inch (40 x 30–cm) rectangle with the long side facing you.

Spread the softened butter over top of the dough, leaving a ½-inch (1.3-cm) strip along the top, then sprinkle the spiced brown sugar over the top of the butter and press down into the butter with your hands. Brush the bare ½-inch (1.3-cm) strip with a bit of water. Roll the dough away from you into a log (try to maintain even thickness throughout). Pinch to seal.

Using a serrated knife or string, slice the log into 12 equal-sized pieces. Place the rolls cut side up into the prepared pan, then cover lightly with plastic wrap and place into a warm place to rise for 30 to 45 minutes, or until nearly doubled in size. Preheat the oven to 350°F (175°C).

(continued)

CREAM CHEESE GLAZE

1 cup (120 g) confectioners' sugar

¾ cup (174 g) cream cheese, softened

½ tsp vanilla extract

CREAM CHEESE GLAZE

While the rolls rise and the oven preheats, make the cream cheese glaze. Place the confectioners' sugar, cream cheese and vanilla in a medium mixing bowl and beat together using a hand mixer until smooth. Cover and set aside.

BAKING THE PUMPKIN ROLLS

Carefully remove the plastic covering the rolls and put the rolls in the oven to bake for about 25 minutes (they should reach an internal temperature of 200°F [95°C] on a kitchen thermometer). Add the cream cheese glaze to the buns while they're still hot.

THE FLUFFIEST RED VELVET ROLLS

Why does everything seem to taste that much better when it is a bright, fun color? These red velvet rolls are soft, pillowy and laced with a delicate chocolate flavor. They are swirled with a classic brown sugar and cinnamon filling and topped with a rich cream cheese frosting, making these a true hybrid dessert!

MAKES 12 ROLLS

RED VELVET DOUGH
¾ cup (180 ml) whole milk, warmed

2¼ tsp (7 g) instant yeast

¼ cup (50 g) white sugar

1 large egg

1 large egg yolk

5 tbsp (75 ml) unsalted butter, melted

1 tbsp (15 ml) gel or liquid red food coloring

3 cups (360 g) all-purpose flour, plus more for dusting

3 tbsp (16 g) cocoa powder, sifted

½ tsp table salt

CINNAMON FILLING
¾ cup (165 g) packed dark brown sugar

2 tbsp (16 g) cinnamon

6 tbsp (85 g) unsalted butter, softened

MAKING THE DOUGH

In the bowl of a stand mixer, whisk together by hand the milk, yeast, sugar, egg, egg yolk, melted butter and food coloring.

In a small mixing bowl, whisk together the flour, cocoa and salt. Add to the stand mixer bowl, then use a large wooden spoon to mix together until a shaggy dough forms. Fit the stand mixer with the dough hook and turn it on to medium. Beat the dough for about 15 minutes, or until the dough is smooth, elastic and tacky.

Transfer the dough to a large greased bowl, cover with plastic wrap, then place in a warm area to rise for 1 to 2 hours, or until the dough is doubled in size.

FILLING, ROLLING AND CUTTING THE RED VELVET ROLLS

In a small mixing bowl, whisk together the brown sugar and cinnamon. Set aside.

Prepare a 9 x 13–inch (23 x 33–cm) pan with cooking spray and parchment. Punch down the risen dough, then turn it out onto a lightly floured work surface, and roll the dough into a 16 x 12–inch (40 x 30–cm) rectangle with the long side facing you.

Spread the softened butter over the top of the dough, leaving a ½-inch (1.3-cm) strip along the top, then sprinkle the cinnamon mixture over the top of the butter and press down into the butter with your hands. Brush the bare ½-inch (1.3-cm) strip with a bit of water. Roll the dough away from you into a log (try to maintain even thickness throughout). Pinch to seal.

Using a serrated knife or string, slice the log into 12 equal-sized pieces. Place the rolls cut side up into the prepared pan, then cover lightly with plastic wrap and set in a warm place to rise for 30 to 45 minutes, or until nearly doubled in size.

Preheat the oven to 350°F (175°C).

(continued)

THE FLUFFIEST RED VELVET ROLLS (CONTINUED)

CREAM CHEESE GLAZE

1 cup (120 g) confectioners' sugar

¾ cup (180 g) cream cheese, softened

½ tsp vanilla extract

CREAM CHEESE GLAZE

While the rolls rise and the oven preheats, make the cream cheese glaze. In a medium mixing bowl, combine all of the cream cheese glaze ingredients and beat together using a hand mixer until smooth. Cover and set aside.

BAKING THE RED VELVET ROLLS

Carefully remove the plastic covering the rolls and put them in the oven to bake for about 25 minutes (they should reach an internal temperature of 200°F [95°C] on a kitchen thermometer). Add the cream cheese glaze to the buns while they're still hot.

ACKNOWLEDGMENTS

To my partner in crime and the love of my life, Sean: Thank you for being the person who has supported me from the beginning of this journey, and continues to keep me grounded while simultaneously lifting me up. Thank you for helping me through my long and rough days, and, more importantly, thank you for bringing me my daily Diet Coke.

To my mom, who first introduced me to the love of baking: Thank you for "taste testing" all my terrible Easy-Bake-Oven creations as a child, and thank you for continuing to be my ultimate taste tester, through both the good and the bad. Thank you for giving me the unconditional love and encouragement I have needed, and for always being my number-one cheerleader.

To my dad, who gave me both his creativity gene and his work ethic: You have taught me what excellence is, and what it means to work hard to achieve your dreams and goals.

Thank you to all my amazing family and friends, who have made this process even more special thanks to all of their affirmations and encouragement. Specifically, to Sarah, who happily devours the extreme amounts of food I give her on a weekly basis. And to Courtney, for giving me the encouragement and confidence I needed to begin food blogging in the first place.

I would like to thank Page Street Publishing for giving me the opportunity of a lifetime in creating this book. Specifically, I would like to give a huge thank you to Emily Taylor and Franny Donington. Thank you, Emily, for seeing something special in me and helping me start this book. And thank you to Franny for being the massive support that I needed to finish this book.

Finally, I can't even begin to thank my followers enough. Without you all, I wouldn't be where I am today. You all have given me the opportunity to follow my lifelong dream of making baking my career. The level of support and love I have felt from my followers and fellow food bloggers on the Internet is, simply put, incredible.

ABOUT THE AUTHOR

Amie MacGregor is a food blogger, recipe developer and food photographer who is the creator of Food Duchess. Originally on track to have a career in business, Amie received her degree in finance, with a focus on personal financial planning, before changing directions and taking a leap of faith into her lifelong passion of baking. Amie has been featured in *Sweet Dreams* magazine, *Modern Texas Living*, thefeedfeed.com and The Bake Feed's Instagram. She was born and raised in Edmonton, Alberta, Canada.

INDEX